BIBLIOGRAPHY & MEMOIR
OF
SIR ADOLPHUS WILLIAM WARD

T0371561

Lafayette, photographer.

Emery Walker ph. sc.

A. W. Ward.

A BIBLIOGRAPHY

OF

SIR ADOLPHUS WILLIAM WARD

1837-1924

By A. T. BARTHOLOMEW

WITH

A MEMOIR

BY

T. F. TOUT

CAMBRIDGE

AT THE UNIVERSITY PRESS

MCMXXVI

CAMBRIDGE
UNIVERSITY PRESS

University Printing House, Cambridge CB2 8BS, United Kingdom

Cambridge University Press is part of the University of Cambridge.

It furthers the University's mission by disseminating knowledge in the pursuit of education, learning and research at the highest international levels of excellence.

www.cambridge.org
Information on this title: www.cambridge.org/9781107560161

First published 1926
First paperback edition 2015

A catalogue record for this publication is available from the British Library

ISBN 978-1-107-56016-1 Paperback

CONTENTS

PREFATORY NOTE

MY FATHER desired that no formal biography of himself should be written after his death. But he left instructions that a bibliography of his writings should be printed in the hope that it might be of service to students: and he expressed a wish that Mr A. T. Bartholomew, of Peterhouse and the University Library, would undertake the somewhat laborious task of preparing it for Press.

To the Bibliography which we owe to Mr Bartholomew's affection and care, it seemed good to prefix the Memoir, instinct with truth and understanding, which Professor T. F. Tout, my father's friend and colleague at Manchester, wrote at the request of the British Academy.

To the Council of the British Academy I would express my thanks for allowing the Memoir, with some corrections and additions, to be here reprinted from its *Proceedings*. I need not formally thank Professor Tout and Mr Bartholomew, for I know that what they have done has been a labour of love.

A. C. T. BARNES

Bishop's Croft
Harborne, Birmingham
April 1926

SIR ADOLPHUS WILLIAM WARD

1837–1924

ADOLPHUS WILLIAM WARD was born at Netley Cottage, Hampstead, on December 2, 1837, and was the second son of John Ward, C.B., and his wife Caroline Bullock. John Ward's father, another John Ward, had been Collector of Customs at East Cowes, and his mother was a sister of Thomas Arnold of Rugby, whose father had preceded the elder John Ward in his collectorship. The younger John had at one time co-operated with his uncle in editing a shortlived newspaper, but was at the time of Adolphus' birth an inspector of prisons. When his son was less than three years old, John Ward was sent to Germany on diplomatic missions which resulted in his establishment there for the rest of his working life. He was between 1845 and 1860 Consul-General at Leipzig, between 1860 and 1870 Consul-General at Hamburg, and finally Minister-Resident to the Hanse Towns. The record of his official work in Germany is preserved in the manuscripts of John Ward, bequeathed by his son to Peterhouse, where they are open to the inspection of historical students. Some of his reminiscences were published in 1872 as *Experiences of a Diplomatist*. Adolphus Ward had two brothers and two sisters. His elder brother, John, became a judge in India and died in early middle life. His younger brother, now Sir William Ward, K.C.M.G., entered the British consular service, and at the time of his retirement was Consul-General at Hamburg. His elder sister married, and left one daughter, who became the wife of Sir Arthur Schuster, late Foreign Secretary of the Royal Society.

The threefold connexions with official service under the Crown, with the Arnold clan and with Germany, had permanent results on Adolphus Ward's attitude throughout life. Residence at Leipzig through his early years made him as familiar with the German speech, literature, and modes of thought as with those of his own land. His early schooling was all in Germany. It began at a preparatory school in Berlin, where his father was sent on a mission. From 1845 to 1853 he was successively at the Nikolaischule at Leipzig, which he described as a 'gymnasium of the old type,' the Blochmann-Vitzthum Institut at Dresden, where he acquired the beginnings of his zest for history from W. Herbst, 'the teacher,' he wrote long afterwards, 'to whom I owe a debt of gratitude which I have cherished through life.' After he was sixteen, his education became purely English. This English education began in 1853 at Bury St Edmunds Grammar School, at a time when Dr J. W. Donaldson, a classical scholar of remarkable attainments, was its head master. He was greatly influenced by his head master, whom he described later 'as a critical scholar of genius and as a teacher unforgettable.' From Bury school he was admitted as a pensioner at Peterhouse, Cambridge, on May 23, 1855. Travelled contemporaries said that he 'looked like a German corps-student,' but he soon made his mark in college society. He graduated in 1859 with a first class in the Classical Tripos, doing especially well in ancient history. He was elected in 1861 to a fellowship which he retained until his marriage, in 1879, with his cousin, Adelaide Laura, daughter of the Rev. T. B. Lancaster. For the first few years his occupations varied considerably. He entered the Inner Temple in 1860 and was called to the Bar in 1866. He never attempted to practise in the profession of the law. He was in succession a lecturer at Peterhouse, a temporary examiner in the Education Office, and assistant to George Ramsay, Professor of Humanity at Glasgow. In 1866 his line of work was permanently determined by his appointment as Professor of History and English Language and Literature at Owens College, Manchester. He remained at Manchester until 1897. Then followed a brief interlude of comparative rest in London from 1897 to 1900. From 1900 to his death he was Master of Peterhouse. Accordingly his active career divides itself between his thirty-two years in Manchester and the twenty-four years after his return to Cambridge.

When Ward went to Manchester, Owens College had outlived the troubles of its early youth, but was still a new and struggling institution. Its students were few in number, young in years, and could only obtain academic status by preparing for the external degrees of the University of London. The courses for these stood in no subject in any direct relation to the teaching at Manchester, and gave little opportunity for specialization in either History or English. Despite these hampering limitations, Ward's teaching stimulated the interest of his students and made a deep impression upon those who came under his influence. He soon began to take the lead in matters of policy. He was one of the four professors who in 1875 issued a pamphlet advocating the erection of Owens College into an independent degree-giving university. After five years of agitation the scheme was adopted by the Privy Council in a radically different form from that which had been in the minds of its promoters. To meet the opposition of Leeds and Liverpool, the compromise of a 'Federal University' was, perhaps too easily, accepted. In 1880 the Victoria University was established with its seat in Manchester and with Owens College as its first constituent college; but other colleges could be taken in, and ultimately University College, Liverpool, and the Yorkshire College, Leeds, were also included.

Ward was disappointed at the compromise, but did his best to make the new university a success. Henceforth administration divided his interests with teaching and writing, and, as time went on, affairs made an increasing demand on his energies. As first chairman of the Board of Studies he was largely responsible for the degree courses of the new university. In particular he organized an Honours School of History on lines that have never been substantially departed from. He acted as Vice-Chancellor from 1886 to 1890 and again from 1894 to 1896. For fifteen years he continued to bear the triple burden of his chair, but after 1880 he obtained some relief by the appointment of a separate Professor of English Philology in the person of T. N. Toller, henceforward his intimate friend. He continued, however, to be responsible for both English Literature and the whole of History until his appointment, in 1889, as Principal of Owens College. He remained until 1897 a Professor of History, and gave a course every year on Roman history until the claims of administration forced him to renounce teaching altogether.

It was in the latter part of his dual professorship that Ward's best work as a teacher was done. He lectured for a prodigious number of hours on a great variety of subjects. Yet he took immense pains with all his courses, making a point of writing out each lecture fully and reading it directly from the manuscript. These manuscripts he was always altering and improving, so that each course became essentially new. His style of exposition was like that of his books, but his strong personality and majestic presence made his lectures still more impressive and stimulating than his written word. His formal method of teaching hardly favoured personal contact with the student, but all his more promising pupils had good cause to realize his interest in their welfare, and his zeal to help them in their careers. It was always his special glory that he communicated to his abler pupils a touch of his enthusiasm for letters and his zeal for the advancement of knowledge. His powerful character impressed every listener; his high-mindedness made contact with him an inspiration; and his courtesy and old-world exquisiteness of manner set a standard rare in modern life. To help a pupil gave him real pleasure. His intense zest for his subject was a stimulus even to the most sluggish. His qualities came out with particular force in his lectures on English literature, at which his audiences were very large. Alike in literature and in history, he attracted to himself able pupils who, under his inspiration, attained distinction in both these lines of study. But even more remarkable is the testimony to his abiding influence on students whose later careers were in no wise directed towards his own lines of work.

Ward was universally recognized as one of the strong men of the College, and when, in 1889, Dr Greenwood resigned the Principalship, he became his successor almost as a matter of course. He retained this office until 1897. During these eight years Ward put himself at the head of every new movement. In nearly every case he succeeded in carrying through his ideas. An early friend of the higher education of women, he secured for women, admitted slowly and rather grudgingly to Owens College, the exercise there of the rights of equal studentship which had been given them in the charter of the University. He took a keen interest in the development of the training department for the education of teachers for both primary and secondary schools. He promoted the extension of the college buildings, the development of new departments, and the increase of the staff. An inspiring address to the students led to the formation of the Manchester University Settlement.

Ward was as much absorbed in the details of administration as in the general direction of policy. He was indefatigable in attending boards and committees. He strove to bring together the various activities of the College into a common focus. The generous and charming hospitality exercised by him and Mrs Ward made their home in Fallowfield a real social centre. But his ceaseless preoccupation in policy, propaganda, and endless detail and routine, wore out his strength and undermined his health. His strong constitution withstood more than one dangerous illness, but in 1897 he determined to resign his post. His retirement was marked by general demonstrations of devotion such as few men have been able to inspire. The two rebuffs which he took most to heart were his failure to persuade the University to establish degrees in theology, and the frustration of his endeavour to put the relations of the College and the Infirmary on a sound basis. He had the satisfaction of seeing these questions settled within a few years of his resignation. He was anxious to play his part in every side of the life he saw around him. Though keeping aloof from practical politics, he was and remained a keen Liberal of a rather old-fashioned sort. He was a zealous churchman, and interested in the broader aspects of all religious questions. It was in recognition of his share in the life of the community that the Corporation of Manchester elected him to the honorary freedom of the city—an appropriate recognition of his services.

In 1897 Dr and Mrs Ward left Manchester and settled down at Kensington. Ill-health still pursued him, but he was not the man to rest, even in retirement. New responsibilities crowded upon him, from which he would not shrink. He became governor of various educational bodies, including the Royal Holloway College, of which his only daughter was a student. He held the Ford Lectureship in English History at Oxford and the presidency of the Royal Historical Society, an honour which he humorously suggested came to him because 'having lately resigned a very busy administrative position, I was doubtless supposed to have a good deal of leisure at my command.' It was characteristic of him that his first presidential address ended with a plea for the establishment of a school of advanced historical training in London, which has since been happily realized. However, after three years, Peterhouse made an irresistible demand on his services. In 1900 he gladly accepted election to the Mastership of his old College, and left London for Cambridge.

The last stage of Ward's career now began, and was extended to a quarter of a century. He had not lost sight of Cambridge during his long absence. He held his fellowship up to 1873 and in 1872 he had published *Suggestions Towards the Establishment of a History Tripos* there, which perhaps bore more practical fruit under his direction in Manchester than in Cambridge itself. In 1884 he had proceeded Litt.D. and in 1891 Peterhouse made him an Honorary Fellow. A year later reminiscences of his undergraduate days appeared in a short-lived college periodical called the *Grayling*, which reflect with charming grace and sincerity the keenness of his memory and the freshness of his enthusiasm for his old College. Such a man was the last person in the world to look upon the headship of a small college as a place of comfortable retirement, and he at once threw himself into the activities of the College and the University. The traditions of a headship were against resuming his teaching, but he found many informal ways of lending a helping hand, and he was as eager as he had been in Manchester to encourage original study and research. He ruled over Peterhouse with a kindly autocracy that greatly conduced to its prosperity. So far as the restricted field allowed, he made Peterhouse a centre of historical study, and his encouragement of advanced work was in no wise limited to his own College. He brought in new blood while carefully fostering domestic merit; he transformed the College and gave it prestige and new ideas; he made it as good, of its kind and size, as any college in the University. He was at his happiest in all personal relations, and the open-handed and genial hospitality dispensed from Peterhouse Lodge made it a social centre whose influence was felt far beyond the College and University.

Ward did important work for the University. He was from an early stage an active member of the Council of the Senate, and was in 1901 called upon to act as Vice-Chancellor, though ill-health compelled him to refuse re-election at the expiration of his first year of office. In general academic politics he was not always able to exercise the dominating influence which he established over his own College. In some quarters he was at first looked upon with suspicion as a revolutionary from a new university, though greater knowledge soon dispelled this illusion. He found that the time was not ripe for the radical measures which he desired and used his influence to shape such moderate reforms as were possible. Thus in 1905 he successfully advocated the separation of the Economic from the Historical Tripos, a course which was probably to the interest of both subjects. When in 1908 the History Tripos was reformed, he pleaded almost passionately for the compulsory study of universal history, but failed to carry his point. His best service to history at Cambridge was, however, to be found in the help which he delighted to give to all advanced work and research. The remarkable development of the serious study of quite recent history in Cambridge owes much to his example and encouragement. He was, too, at his best on some of the special syndicates, notably on the Library and Press Syndicates, to both of which he devoted an immensity of time and thought. In the former he pressed for acquisitions in continental literature, especially on the historical and literary sides. When the Acton Library was presented to the University, Ward was one of the committee which drew up the scheme of classification, and personally interested himself in its cataloguing and arrangement. On the Press Syndicate, of which he was a member between 1905 and 1919, and chairman for the greater part of the period, his influence was supreme.

His work at Cambridge never prevented Ward from keeping up old obligations and attachments. A remarkable instance of his devotion to the institutions with which he had once been associated is seen in his enduring affection for Bury School, of which he was in later years a governor. His loyalty to Manchester remained as strong as his piety and affection for Cambridge. As a member of the Court, the supreme governing body of Manchester University, he closely followed all movements there. When Liverpool started an agitation for the dissolution of the Federal Victoria University, Ward's vigorous return to the ideals of 1875 did much to make Manchester follow the lead of Liverpool, and to ensure the dissolution of the Federal University which only taught through its colleges. With the establishment of the independent University of Manchester in 1903, including a faculty of theology, he saw the accomplishment of one of his chief ambitions. Of that University Ward is, more than any other man, the true founder. He followed its developments with unabated interest until the end, and bequeathed to it a legacy which has been appropriately assigned to the subvention of the publication of works of scholarship and research in History and English Literature by the Manchester University Press. He also left the bulk of his books and a legacy of £1050 to Peterhouse. The money has been used by the College to equip the Ward Library for students in History and English Literature, in which his books are now separately preserved. A bequest of £1000, left to the College by his wife, has been devoted to establish the 'Lady Ward Scholarship' in History.

Recognition of Ward's services had already flowed in from many quarters. Glasgow admitted him to the honorary degree of LL.D., and in 1895 he became honorary Litt.D. of Victoria University. He was also made an honorary Ph.D. in Leipzig. In 1911 he became a Knight of the Prussian Order of the Crown. In 1913 he was dubbed knight by King George V. He was President of the Spenser Society, President of the Royal Historical Society from 1899 to 1901, of the Chetham Society from 1901 to 1915, President of the English Goethe Society from 1911 until shortly before his death, and Vice-President of the Historical Association from its beginning in 1906.

In 1902 Ward was nominated in the charter both a fellow and a member of the Council of the British Academy. In 1908–10 he again served on its Council: from 1911 to 1913 he was its President, and again sat on the Council from 1913 to 1915. In the absence of Lord Bryce he acted as President of the London meeting of the International Historical Congress in April 1913. He was never more happy than when discharging the duties of president of a learned body. The unfailing dignity, urbanity, and patience with which he directed the proceedings of the London Congress largely contributed to the success of that gathering.

Up to now we have traced Ward's career as teacher and administrator. But the remarkable thing about him is that with responsibilities in these two relations which might well have fully occupied the energies of an ordinary strong man, he pursued at the same time the life of a scholar and writer. He published very little until he was over thirty, but for the rest of his life a stream of lectures, articles, pamphlets, and books continued to attest his immense and varied literary activity. This stream never ceased, though it flowed with comparative slowness during the strenuous years of his Manchester Principalship. It continued unabated until his last publications appeared after his death at the age of eighty-six. Some idea of the bulk and variety of this output may be seen from the complete bibliography which Mr A. T. Bartholomew has printed in the present volume[1].

It is characteristic of Ward's immense learning, strength, and vitality that he ever found his chief delight in turning from teaching and administration to literary production. All through his long career as a writer he carried the dualism of his Manchester chair into his private work. In one of his earliest published addresses, in 1866, he remarked humorously that the subjects for which he was responsible encouraged 'a perhaps naturally truant disposition to the systematic dissipation of such energies as it possessed.' However this may be, the 'dissipation' became so firmly fixed that it remained with him till the end, and the rival claims of English literature and ancient

[1] Besides this, reference may be made to Dr T. A. Walker, *A Peterhouse Bibliography*, pp. 123–124 (1924).

and modern history continued to divide his attention. Yet few men have dealt so successfully with so wide a field of knowledge. His literary and historical writings have won him the respect and admiration of scholars in many different fields. In an age of specialism it was inevitable that specialists should pick holes in some of his books. But a prodigious memory, unremitting application, remarkable quickness in work, and rare breadth of interests combined to make all his varied output scholarly, solid, and important. In some ways he was hampered by a literary style which smacked somewhat of his German education and was a little lacking in simplicity, directness, and charm. The result was that effective and impressive as he was as a lecturer, his elaborate style made him occasionally somewhat difficult to follow in cold print.

Ward's earlier publications were largely literary, and the strongest of them centred round the history of the drama. He was not only a learned historian of dramatic origins, but he was until middle life an enthusiastic playgoer, and for many years was the dramatic critic of the *Manchester Guardian*. The wide scope of his dramatic knowledge is best revealed in his first single undertaking on a large scale, his *History of English Dramatic Literature to the Death of Queen Anne*, published in two volumes in 1875. No other book in the language had hitherto attempted to cover this immense field. As a study of origins, it has been superseded by later works. But as a conspectus of the whole subject, it is a book of enormous labour and of solid value. In a second edition, published in three volumes in 1899, Ward valiantly strove to bring it up to the level of the advance made by scholarship and added considerably to its original scope. An even wider survey was made in the article on the *Drama*, contributed to the ninth edition of the *Encyclopaedia Britannica*, which in an enlarged and revised form still held its place in the current eleventh edition, published in 1910. His other contributions to that Encyclopaedia were mainly on dramatists and other dramatic subjects, including Pantomime. Among his numerous editions of old plays, that of Marlowe's *Dr Faustus* and Greene's *Friar Bungay*, first published in 1878 and since enlarged in numerous later editions, is a characteristic example of recondite learning and unflagging industry.

This is only one example of Ward's unwearied energy as a literary editor. Of his other editorial labours may be mentioned, as the earliest of the type, his edition of *Pope's Works* in 1869 for Macmillan's *Globe Series*; while the *Poems of George Crabbe* (1905–1907) and the *Knutsford Edition of the Works of Mrs Gaskell* (1906) belonged to his late Cambridge period. His short biographies of *Chaucer* (1880) and *Dickens* (1882) in Macmillan's *English Men of Letters* are further illustrations of the width of his range. *The Life of Dickens* is among the most successful of his shorter books. His edition of the voluminous *Poems of John Byrom*, the Manchester Jacobite, nonjuring bishop and physician (two volumes, 1894–5), was completed in 1912 by a third volume, issued, as he said, not only as the duty of the president of the Chetham Society, but also as a 'slight labour of love' for Byrom's native town. We must deal later with his last elaborate service to letters, both as editor and contributor of the *Cambridge History of English Literature*. But we must not forget his lectures before the British Academy on *The Tercentenary of Milton* (1908) and on *Shakespeare and the Makers of Virginia* (1919).

Ward's knowledge of literature in many tongues was exceedingly wide. He kept up his classical scholarship to the end. He spoke German like a native and was deeply read in German literature. His facility of speech in French was almost equally complete. His zest and appreciation for good poetry and prose in all languages were intense. But in his writings he generally tended towards the historical rather than the critical side, and was at his best when he did so. It is difficult, therefore, to draw the line between his literary and historical writings. This is particularly the case with his numerous lectures, articles, and contributions to newspapers and periodicals. Among these may be specially mentioned his frequent articles in the *Saturday Review*, the *Manchester Guardian*, the *Cornhill Magazine*, *Macmillan's Magazine*, and the *Quarterly* and *Edinburgh Reviews*. Specimens of these have been brought together, along with reprints of many occasional papers of a more elaborate character, in the five volumes of his *Collected Papers: Historical, Literary, Travel and Miscellaneous*, published as a freewill recognition of his services by the Cambridge University Press in 1921. The number of these volumes could have been largely increased from his published articles without damage to their quality. But as they stand they illustrate sufficiently the width of his range and the variety of his interests. Special reference may well be made to his papers on travel, for until middle life Ward was an eager traveller, and delighted to write and speak of his wanderings in historic lands.

Ward's contributions to historical literature began late. The first was a work of great labour, the translation into English of Ernst Curtius's *History of Greece*, in five volumes, issued between 1868 and 1873. The first independent book on an historical subject was his short treatise on the *Counter Reformation*, published in 1889 in Longman's *Epochs of Church History*. Numerous occasional papers and articles showed that he was already a serious worker in the historical field. The history of Germany was always a study near to his heart, and an early ambition, encouraged by the great Lappenberg, had been to write a systematic history of the Hanseatic league. But this, he tells us, 'remained a vision,' though he long hoped to make German history his main study. It was generally believed in the seventies and eighties that he was accumulating materials for a general history of Germany, and it is certain that he had qualifications possessed by few Englishmen for this stupendous task. But the increasing claims of official work and the distractions of occasional publications prevented the realization of this task even on a small scale, though the three useful volumes on *Germany 1815–1890*, published by him in the *Cambridge Historical Series* between 1916 and 1918, represent a very thorough working up of the more recent periods to which his interest had gradually become transferred. It followed that his historical output consisted mainly of short pieces of work, papers, articles, lectures, and monographs, which were always learned, weighty, and valuable, but were not sufficiently closely related to each other to help towards the production of any one great undertaking. The majority of them treated either of German history, the history of the Renaissance, or the history of England in the seventeenth and eighteenth centuries. Much valuable work on the statesmen of the seventeenth century is contained in his three hundred contributions to the *Dictionary of National Biography*, amounting to two-thirds of a volume of the original edition of the work and including long and solid articles on Queen Anne and Charles II. He was one of the founders of the *English Historical Review* and among its most generous and untiring friends. His contributions to its pages, including very numerous reviews, came with unfailing regularity, and his last review in it was published after his death. Of his smaller books it is enough to mention his *House of Austria in the Thirty Years' War* (1869), *Sir Henry Wotton: A Biographical Sketch* (1898), his Ford Lectures on *Great Britain and Hanover: Some Aspects of the Personal Union* (1899), *The Electress Sophia and the Hanoverian Succession* (1903), and *The Period of Congresses* and *Securities of Peace* in the S.P.C.K. *Helps for Students of History*.

Having deeply at heart the building up of schools of history and the encouragement and direction of historical investigation, Ward was always disposed to throw his energies into any co-operative enterprises of scholarship. He was apprenticed in discipline of this sort through his relations to such undertakings as the *Dictionary of National Biography* and the *English Historical Review*. Just before the time of his final return to Cambridge accident involved him in an active part in another work of co-operative scholarship, which was to determine his chief literary activity in the last quarter of a century of his life. Lord Acton had designed and mapped out a co-operative history of modern Europe in twelve volumes, each of which was to centre round some historical fact of signal importance as the central idea round which individual developments were to be grouped, not accidentally but of reasoned purpose. He had enlisted contributors, collected articles, and drawn up a general plan. But the realization of so idealistic a scheme was beyond his strength, and his fatal illness took place before anything could be published. Ward was early interested in the enterprise and, with characteristic loyalty, took up the burden which Acton had been unable to bear. He was appointed Editor-in-chief in association with the late Dr (afterwards Sir) George Prothero and Mr (now Sir) Stanley Leathes. The future of the undertaking was soon secured. Between

1902 and 1911 the fourteen large volumes of the *Cambridge Modern History* were duly published.

Ward's colleagues in the direction of the Cambridge Histories, Sir Stanley Leathes and Dr G. P. Gooch, have well described in print his editorial methods[1]. They were remarkable for their meticulousness and thoroughness. Every section was read and re-read by him personally and every contributor was kept in close touch with the direction. Ward's power of carrying things through triumphed over the remissness of the most dilatory of his contributors. With all his unwearied attention to detail, he kept well before him the wide ideals of Acton, and if the outcome was not quite what Acton had hoped for, it resulted in an extremely useful and valuable compendium of modern history on a large and noble scale, based upon sound knowledge of the best sources, and almost over-flowing in the elaboration and completeness of its details. Ward was not only chief editor, but one of the most fertile contributors, almost entirely on German history.

The remarkable success of the *Cambridge Modern History* encouraged the University Press to other similar ventures in co-operative synthesis. The first of these was the *Cambridge History of English Literature*, which was issued in fourteen volumes between 1907 and 1916. In this work Ward was again chief editor with the late Mr A. R. Waller, of the University Press, as his colleague. To its later volumes Ward made numerous contributions, dealing with very varied phases of the subject, and ranging from the origins of the drama to the historians of the nineteenth century. The whole work was perhaps less uniform in quality than the *Modern History*, but some parts of it are of remarkable excellence. Other works of the same kind followed, such as the *Cambridge Ancient*

---

[1] *The Cambridge Historical Journal*, vol. I, No. 2.

History and the *Cambridge Mediaeval History.* With neither of these had Ward any direct connexion, but they met with his approval and backing on the Press Syndicate. Unlike the series for which Ward was responsible, they have not yet (1925) been completed. It was otherwise with the last of his Cambridge co-operative histories. *The Cambridge History of British Foreign Policy,* edited by Ward and Dr G. P. Gooch, appeared in three volumes between 1922 and 1923. It was a wonderful achievement, designed by a man over eighty and carried through by the time he was eighty-five. Dr Gooch's zealous and loyal friendship relieved him of some of the editorial drudgery, but editorial habits were too firmly established for him to delegate many of his labours. Once more he was con-tributor as well as editor. Besides an elaborate general introductory survey, he wrote two chapters, one on 'The Schleswig-Holstein Question' and the other on 'Greece and the Ionian Islands.' The former section contains some of the best and most original work he ever did, for it was largely based on the material brought together by his father, whose chief distinction as a diplomatist rested on his handling of the Schleswig-Holstein question between 1857 and 1862. So bold was John Ward's chief minute on this subject that it was refused publication through the ordinary official channel.

Thus in his last as in his earliest work the influence on Ward of his German masters was very strong. He was one of the earliest and best of the interpreters of German scholarship to English readers. But his love of thorough-ness and detail never blinded him to the more human aspects of history. In this he was a true disciple of his great-uncle Dr Arnold. Moreover, much of his written work, like that of his friend Freeman, was as didactic and educational in its purpose as were his academic lectures. In this way he shared with Freeman in helping forward the creation of an English school of historical scholarship.

All through his life Ward was anxious to do all that was in his power to emphasize friendly relations between the land of his birth and that of his early education. His constant social and literary relations with German scholars were not simply for the sake of scholarship but were consciously directed to this end. These intimacies and his profound appreciation of German learning and scholarship made him feel with great acuteness the rupture of these ties as a result of the Great War. He convinced himself, however, of the righteousness of the allied cause, and bore disappointment with characteristic fortitude. His attitude to the great struggle is well brought out in a striking address, *Founder's Day in War Time*, which he gave in 1917 on the occasion of his last visit to Manchester.

During the years immediately succeeding the peace, Ward's physical powers began slowly to fail. Increasing deafness made it difficult for him to serve on committees, and forced the most hospitable of men playfully to beg the indulgence of his guests. But he still kept up his life-long habit of constant toil, and remained to the last as eager as ever to promote learning and help forward the young scholar. The end came almost suddenly at Peterhouse Lodge on June 19, 1924. He was buried in the church-yard of Cherry Hinton, where so many of his predecessors at Peterhouse lie interred. Lady Ward did not long outlive him. There had been no flaw in their companionship of five and forty years: its only abiding grief was the loss of their firstborn infant son. Complete interdependence made of their married life a beautiful and rare perfection. Her comradeship with her husband helped not only him but all who knew him. Religious in the best sense, she carried her high principles, her sympathy, and her generosity of act and judgment into every relation of life. Frail in health during her latter years, she yet survived him with courage. But as a friend well said, 'It was like her to hasten after him.' Within six months she died at Bishop's Croft, Harborne, near Birmingham, where she had gone to live with their only daughter, the wife of Dr E. W. Barnes, who, soon after Ward's death, had been made Bishop of Birmingham. She was buried by her husband's side at Cherry Hinton.

Ward's long life of eighty-six years was packed full of achievement. As a scholar he won distinction in widely different literary and historical fields. As a teacher and writer he was a stimulus to many generations of disciples, some now grown old, who have achieved fame in very different walks of life. He was a leader in the vindication of the right of history and modern literature to obtain academic recognition, and of the claim of women to share fully in the opportunities of men to obtain higher education. As an academic administrator he was foremost among the makers of a new university and the reformers of an old one. But, great as was his achievement, it counts for little as compared with the personality and character which inspired it. Critics might complain that his scholarship with all its width was seldom ultimate, that his academic leadership was sometimes tempered by prudent opportunism, and that his devotion to detail sometimes obscured the basic principles which inspired him. But there could be only one opinion of the man. His very presence was an inspiration and made him an ideal leader. Tall, dignified, gravely magnificent in manner, he bore, in middle life, a striking physical resemblance to his cousin, Matthew Arnold, though few men were more unlike in their general attitude of mind. He was sometimes said to have inherited the manners of the diplomatist of the older school, courteous and urbane but somewhat formal, aloof, and haughty. But this was a very superficial view of one of the most kindly, friendly, and sympathetic of men. His stately manner could obscure, only to very unseeing eyes, the warmth of his affections and the kindliness and simplicity of his nature. It was these qualities which made him sympathetic with the young, down to the end of his career. Those privileged to know him intimately were constantly inspired by his example to emulate his single-minded devotion to high ideals, his absolute absorption in the work that lay before him, his unselfishness, his disregard of his own ease and comfort, and his scorn for mean and petty issues. Though intolerant of slipshod and unscholarly work, he was never blind to honest merit, and was generous in perceiving in others qualities and methods very different from his own. His private life was singularly happy but uneventful, and he found his best refreshment in the family circle and in the society of a few intimates. But his rare social gifts included a genius for hospitality and friendship which knew little distinction of country, class, or creed. He was as well known in academic circles on the Continent, notably in Germany, as in this country. He kept in touch to the end with a wide and varied acquaintance by means of a vast correspondence for which he always seemed to find time, though he wrote most of his letters with his own hand. In more intimate circles he was, perhaps, rather slow in giving his confidence, but when it was once won, he gave it ungrudgingly and completely. It was well said of him that 'Ward never forgot a friend.' 'Do not be afraid of being sentimental' was advice which he was fond of giving to his Manchester pupils. This touch of emotion was not the least of his attractiveness to those who got near enough to him to realize its strength[1].

[1] In preparing this notice I have made free use of an obituary of Ward in the *Manchester Guardian* of June 20, 1924, for which I was mainly responsible. I have also borrowed something from the obituary notice in *The Times*, clearly written from intimate knowledge, and from the personal sketch by the Master of Emmanuel and Professor W. Emery Barnes of Peterhouse, prefixed to *In Memoriam: Adolphus William Ward*. Cambridge 1924. Among the friends who have helped me with material and advice, I wish specially to thank Mrs E. W. Barnes; and Dr T. A. Walker and Dr Harold Temperley, both of Peterhouse.

T. F. TOUT

TABLE OF PRINCIPAL DATES

1837, Dec. 2. Born at Hampstead.

1855. Entered Peterhouse after earlier education in Germany and at King Edward VI Grammar School, Bury St Edmunds.

1859. Graduated, 1st Class in Classical Tripos.

1861. Fellow of Peterhouse.

1866. Professor of History and of English Language and Literature at the Owens College, Manchester.

1879. Marriage.

1880. Foundation of the Victoria University.

1884. Litt.D. Cambridge.

1886–90, 1894–6. Vice-Chancellor of the Victoria University.

1889. Principal of the Owens College.

1891. Honorary Fellow of Peterhouse.

1895. Honorary Litt.D., Victoria University.

1897. Resigned Principalship.

1899–1901. President of the Royal Historical Society.

1900. Master of Peterhouse.

1901. Vice-Chancellor of the University of Cambridge.

1902. Fellow of the British Academy.

1903. Foundation of the independent University of Manchester.

1911–13. President of the British Academy.

1913. Knighted.

1924, June 19. Died at Cambridge.

NOTE TO THE BIBLIOGRAPHY

FROM the year 1860 until his death in 1924 the late Master of Peterhouse kept a record of his various historical and literary writings as they appeared; and also (in the same book) of the principal lectures, speeches, reports, etc., which he made, whether these were printed or no. This record forms the basis of the following bibliography; and the unprinted items have been included with the printed ones as helping to show the extraordinary extent of his energies and the width of his interests.

In nearly every case the entries have been checked and amplified; various additions have been made; and the whole has been arranged in chronological order. Under each year the arrangement is as follows:

1. Chief works, and published or printed lectures, addresses, etc. In italic type.
2. Contributions to periodical literature. The title prefixed by the author to a contribution is given in italics.
3. Works edited, annotated, or with introduction by A. W. W.
4. Lectures, addresses, speeches, and reports, for the most part neither published nor printed. These are enclosed within square brackets.

I wish to thank Professor T. F. Tout and Mrs E. W. Barnes for reading the proofs of the Bibliography and making many useful suggestions; and Mr A. J. Crow, of the University Library, for valuable help in the work of checking and arrangement.

A. T. BARTHOLOMEW

Cambridge
April 1926

ABBREVIATIONS

Dictionary of National Biography	D.N.B.
English Historical Review	E.H.R.
Manchester Guardian	M.G.
Quarterly Review	Q.R.
Saturday Review	S.R.

A LIST
OF THE WORKS OF
ADOLPHUS WILLIAM WARD

In the case of published books and pamphlets where no place of publication is mentioned London may be assumed.

An asterisk (*) prefixed to an entry signifies that the item so marked is included in *Collected Papers* (1921).

1860

Life of Goethe. With alterations and additions by J. D. Nichol. (M'Kenzie's *Biographical Dictionary.*)

1860–1862

Letters M, N, O. Unrevised. (Dr Wm Smith's *English-Latin Dictionary.*)

1861

The Late Dr Donaldson.   (*Museum*, No. II, July.)

1862

Notice of T. Kock's "Goethii Iphigenia Graece."
      (*Museum*, No. IV, Jan.)

1863

Was Nero a Monster?   (*Museum*, No. XI, Oct.)

**Treves, the Belgic Rome.*   (*Bentley's Miscellany*, Oct.)

The Comic Press in Russia.   (*London Rev.* Feb. 7.)

Prussian Alliances.   (*London Rev.* Feb. 21.)

Prudelwitz and Strudelwitz.   (*S.R.* May 16.)

Stahr's "Life of Lessing." Review of 'G. E. Lessing, sein Leben und seine Werke,' von Adolf Stahr, 2te Ausgabe. 1862.
(*S.R.* May 30.)

A Norseman's Views of Britain and the British. Review of 'A Norseman's Views of Britain and the British,' by A. O. Vinje. 1863. (*S.R.* June 20.)

Prussian Parliamentary Leaders. Review of 'Preussische Landtagsmänner...,' von E. Schmidt-Weissenfels. 1862.
(*S.R.* June 27.)

*Songs of the Thirty Years' War. Review of 'Der dreissigjährige Krieg...,' von Julius Opel und Adolf Cohn. 1862.
(*S.R.* July 11.)

The Jobsiad. Review of 'The Jobsiad, a grotesco-comico-heroic poem, from the German of Carl Arnold Kostüm,' by Charles T. Brooks. 1863. (*S.R.* Aug. 22.)

Goethe's Correspondence with Karl August. Review of 'Briefwechsel des Erzherzogs Karl August von Sachsen-Weimar-Eisenach mit Goethe in den Jahren von 1775 bis 1828.' 2 Bde. 1863.
(*S.R.* Aug. 29.)

Ludwig Uhland. Review of 'Ludwig Uhland, sein Leben und seine Dichtungen,' von Friedrich Notter. 1863.
(*S.R.* Sept. 19.)

*Jacob Grimm. (*S.R.* Oct. 3.)

Social Life in Germany. Review of 'Social life in Munich,' by Edward Wilberforce. 1863.—'German life and manners, as seen in Saxony at the present time,' by Henry Mayhew. 2 vols. 1864. (*S.R.* Dec. 26.)

1864

The Townley Case.   (*Glasgow Medical Journal,* April.)

The Precedence of Edinburgh and Dublin.
(*London Rev.* March 5.)

Pauli's "History of England from 1814," vol. I. Review of 'Geschichte Englands seit den Friedensschlüssen von 1814 und 1815.' Theil I. 1864.   (*London Rev.* July 23.)

Russia under Catharine II and Paul. Review of 'Graf J. J. von Sievers, und Russland zu dessen Zeit.' 1864.
                                                    (*London Rev.* Oct. 22.)

*Tilly. Review of 'Tilly im Dreissigjährigen Kriege,' von Onno Klopp. 1861.   (*S.R.* Jan. 30.)

*The Hanseatic League. Review of 'Histoire Commerciale de la Ligue Hanséatique,' par Émile Worms. 1864.   (*S.R.* Feb. 13.)

Wachsmuth's "History of Hildesheim." Review of 'Geschichte von Hochstift und Stadt Hildesheim,' von Wilhelm Wachsmuth. 1863.   (*S.R.* March 5.)

Schubart and His Contemporaries. Review of 'Schubart und seine Zeitgenossen. Historischer Roman,' von A. E. Brachvogel. 4 Bde. 1864.   (*S.R.* April 9.)

The Danes Sketched by Themselves. Review of 'The Danes sketched by themselves: a series of popular stories by the best Danish authors,' translated by Mrs Bushby. 3 vols. 1864.
                                                    (*S.R.* April 23.)

Day Dreams of a Schoolmaster. Review of 'Day dreams of a schoolmaster,' by D'Arcy W. Thompson. 1864.   (*S.R.* May 7.)

Roman History at Rome. Review of 'L'Histoire Romaine à Rome,' par J. J. Ampère. Tomes III et IV. 1864.   (*S.R.* June 4.)

Keym's "History of the Thirty Years' War." Review of 'Geschichte des Dreissigjährigen Krieges...,' von Franz Keym. 2 Bde. 1863–4.   (*S.R.* July 9.)

*Saint-Napoléon.   (*S.R.* Aug. 20.)

Correspondence of Ludwig Tieck. Review of 'Briefe an Ludwig Tieck...,' von Karl von Höltei. I. und II. Bd. 1864.
                                                    (*S.R.* Sept. 10.)

Shakspeare. A Winter Night's Dream. Review of 'Shakspeare. Ein Winternachtstraum...,' von Karl Kösting. 1864.
(*S.R.* Sept. 17.)

Novum iter Germanicum.   (*S.R.* Oct. 8.)

Cleopatra. Review of 'Cleopatra,' von Adolf Stahr. 1864.
(*S.R.* Nov. 5.)

*Roman Manners under the Earlier Emperors. Review of 'Darstellungen aus der Sittengeschichte Roms in der Zeit von August bis zum Ausgang der Antonine,' von Ludwig Friedländer. I. und II. Theil. 1862–4.   (*S.R.* Nov. 12.)

*The Brothers Grimm. Review of 'Rede auf Wilhelm Grimm, und Rede über das Alter,' von Jacob Grimm. Herausgegeben von Herman Grimm. 1864.   (*S.R.* Dec. 3.)

William the Silent. Review of 'Wilhelm I von Oranien, etc. Aus dem Nachlasse K. L. Klose's, mit einer Würdigung des Oraniers,' von H. Wuttke. 1864.   (*S.R.* Dec. 31.)

1865

Don Carlos and Philip II. Review of 'Don Carlos et Philippe II,' par M. Gachard. 2 tomes.   (*S.R.* Jan. 28.)

Masaniello. Review of 'Masaniello of Naples,' by Mrs Horace Roscoe St John. 1865.   (*S.R.* March 18.)

The Munich Historical Year Book. Review of 'Münchener Historisches Jahrbuch für 1865.' 1865.   (*S.R.* April 15.)

The Warriors of the Thirty Years' War. Review of 'Lives of the Warriors of the Thirty Years' War,' by the Hon. Sir Edward Cust. 1865.   (*S.R.* May 6.)

Don John of Austria. Review of 'Das Leben des Don Juan d'Austria,' von Wilh. Havemann. 1865.   (*S.R.* May 13.)

Molière. Review of 'Molière-Characters,' by Charles Cowden Clarke. 1865.   (*S.R.* May 27.)

The Empire under Ferdinand III. Review of 'Geschichte des deutschen Reiches unter der Regierung Ferdinands III. Nach handschr. Quellen,' von M. Koch. 1. Bd. 1865.
(*S.R.* June 24.)

Ulric of Wirtemberg. Review of 'Ulrich Herzog zu Wirtemberg,' von Bernhard Kugler. 1865.   (*S.R.* July 8.)

Spain from 1788. Review of 'Geschichte Spaniens vom Ausbruch d. franz. Revol. bis auf unsere Tage,' von Hermann Baumgarten. 1. Theil. 1865.   (*S.R.* July 29.)

On the Heights. Review of 'Auf der Höhe...,' von Berthold Auerbach. 1865.   (*S.R.* Aug. 19.)

Maurice de Saxe. Review of 'Maurice de Saxe,' par St. René-Taillandier. 1865.—'Moritz, Graf von Sachsen. Nach archiv. Quellen,' von Karl von Weber. 1863.   (*S.R.* Sept. 2.)

The Intellectual City. Review of 'Die Stadt der Intelligenz,' von Schmidt-Weissenfels. 1865.   (*S.R.* Oct. 7.)

Lübeck.   (*S.R.* Oct. 14.)

Father Arndt. Review of 'Ernst Moritz Arndt, sein Leben und seine Schriften,' von E. Langenberg. 1865.   (*S.R.* Oct. 14.)

A Scottish Family Abroad. Review of 'Our summer in the Harz Forest,' by a Scottish family. 1865.   (*S.R.* Dec. 23.)

1866

National Self-Knowledge. Lecture delivered in the Town Hall, Manchester, Oct. 2. Introductory to the Session of Owens College. Manchester.

Franzisca Hernandez and Franzisco Ortiz. Review of 'Franzisca Hernandez und Frai Franzisco Ortiz...,' von Eduard Boehmer.
(*S.R.* June 30.)

The Foreign Policy of Henry VIII. Review of 'England im Re-
formationszeitalter.' Vier Vorträge von Wilhelm Maurenbrecher. 1866.   (*S.R.* Oct. 6.)

*The Outbreak of the Seven Years' War. Review of 'Die Geheim-
nisse d. Sächs. Cabinets. Ende 1745 bis Ende 1756.' Archivar.
Vorstudien zur Gesch. d. siebenj. Krieges. 2 Bde. 1866.
                                             (*S.R.* Oct. 27.)

Albert I of Habsburg. Review of 'Albrecht I. von Habsburg,
Herzog von Oesterreich und Römischer König,' von J. F.
Alphons Mücke. 1866.   (*S.R.* Nov. 10.)

Charles V and the German Protestants. Review of 'Karl V. u. d.
deutschen Protestanten, 1545–1555,' von Wilh. Maurenbrecher.
                                             (*S.R.* Dec. 8.)

1867

Three Lectures on Germany and German Unity. I. Before 1815;
II. The Germanic Confederation; *III. The North German Federal
State.* Delivered in Memorial Hall, Albert Square, Manchester,
Nov. 13, 20, 27.
                    (*Manchester Examiner*, Nov. 14, 23, 28.)

Agrippina, the Mother of Nero. Review of 'Agrippina die Mutter
Neros' (Bilder aus dem Alterthume), von Adolf Stahr. 1867.
                                             (*S.R.* May 18.)

Anne of Saxony. Review of 'Anna Churfürstin zu Sachsen. Nach
archiv. Quellen,' von K. von Weber. 1865.   (*S.R.* June 1.)

*Abraham a Sancta Clara. Review of 'Abraham a Sancta Clara,'
von Th. G. von Karajan. Vienna, 1867.   (*S.R.* June 15.)

*Ludwig Börne. Review of 'Gesammelte Schriften von Ludwig
Börne.' 12 Bde. 1862.   (*S.R.* June 22.)

The Life of Ritter. Review of 'The life of Ritter, late Professor of Geography in the University of Berlin,' by W. L. Gage. 1867.   (*S.R.* July 13.)

Henry of Valois and Poland in 1572. (First notice.) Review of 'Henri de Valois et la Pologne en 1572,' par le Marquis de Noailles. 3 tomes. 1867.   (*S.R.* Aug. 31.)

Henry of Valois and Poland in 1572. (Second notice.) Review of 'Henri de Valois et la Pologne en 1572,' par le Marquis de Noailles. 3 tomes. 1867.   (*S.R.* Sept. 28.)

The London Theatres.—Artemus Ward as a Lecturer. Two articles.   (*M.G.* Jan. 15.)

Mr Dickens's Reading at the Free-Trade Hall.   (*M.G.* Feb. 4.)

Prince's Theatre: Palgrave Simpson's "Blind Nelly," at Prince's Theatre.   (*M.G.* Feb. 5.)

Prince's Theatre: Tom Taylor's "Nine Points of the Law," at Prince's Theatre.   (*M.G.* Feb. 12.)

Queen's Theatre: Mr Boucicault's "The Great Strike," at Queen's Theatre.   (*M.G.* Feb. 26.)

"King Lear," at Theatre Royal.   (*M.G.* March 8.)

"A Wife's Trials," at Theatre Royal.   (*M.G.* March 12.)

"Othello," at Prince's Theatre.   (*M.G.* March 19.)

Lord Byron's "Manfred," at Prince's Theatre. (*M.G.* March 27.)

Lord Byron's "Manfred," at Prince's Theatre.   (*M.G.* April 9.)

The Rev. Mr Bellew's Readings at the Free-Trade Hall.
                                           (*M.G.* April 29.)

"Hamlet," at Theatre Royal.   (*M.G.* April 30.)

"Much Ado About Nothing," at Theatre Royal.   (*M.G.* May 4.)

"Richard II" and "Jealous Wife," at Theatre Royal.
                                            (*M.G.* May 11.)

J. L. Toole's Sketches from Life at Free-Trade Hall.
                                        (*M.G.* May 13.)

Mr Palgrave Simpson's "Broken Ties" and Mr F. C. Burnand's
  "Blackeyed Susan," at Theatre Royal.   (*M.G.* May 14.)

S. Knowles' "William Tell," at Prince's Theatre.
                                        (*M.G.* May 22.)

Mr Tom Taylor's "The Hidden Hand," at Theatre Royal.
                                        (*M.G.* June 4.)

"Measure for Measure," at Theatre Royal.   (*M.G.* June 24.)

Mr and Mrs Calvert's Farewell at Free-Trade Hall.
                                        (*M.G.* June 24.)

Mr Dion Boucicault's "Flying Scud," at Prince's Theatre.
                                        (*M.G.* June 26.)

Professor Kingsley on the Ancien Régime. Review.
                                        (*M.G.* June 26.)

Goldwin Smith's "Three English Statesmen." Review of 'Three
  English Statesmen: a course of lectures on the political history
  of England,' by Goldwin Smith. 1867.   (*M.G.* July 30.)

The Conservative Banquet.   (*M.G.* Oct. 17.)

Theodore Martin's "King René's Daughter," at Theatre Royal.
                                        (*M.G.* Oct. 30.)

"Much Ado About Nothing," at Theatre Royal.   (*M.G.* Nov. 2.)

"Lady of Lyons," at Theatre Royal.   (*M.G.* Nov. 4.)

Charles Dickens's "David Copperfield," at Theatre Royal.
                                        (*M.G.* Nov. 5.)

Mr Dion Boucicault's "Willow Copse," at Prince's Theatre.
                                        (*M.G.* Nov. 15.)

"Leah," at Theatre Royal.   (*M.G.* Nov. 19.)

Mr H. J. Byron's "The Old Story," at Prince's Theatre.
(*M.G.* Dec. 3.)

G. A'Beckett's "Not Guilty," at Prince's Theatre.
(*M.G.* Dec. 11.)

1868

*The North-Frisian Outlands.   (*Cornhill Mag.* April.)

Pemberton's "History of Monaco." Review of 'The history of
Monaco; past and present,' by H. Pemberton. (*S.R.* June 13.)

Beaumarchais on his Travels. Review of 'Beaumarchais und
Sonnenfels,' von Alfred Ritter von Arneth. 1868.
(*S.R.* June 27.)

The Women of Goethe. Review of 'Goethe's Frauengestalten,' von
Adolf Stahr. 2 Bde. 1865 und 1868.   (*S.R.* July 11.)

Italian Journeys. Review of 'Italian journeys,' by W. D. Howells.
1868.   (*S.R.* Aug. 15.)

*Klopstock and his Friends. Review of 'Briefe von und an Klopstock. Ein Beitrag zur Litteraturgeschichte seiner Zeit.' Mit
erläuternden Anmerkungen herausgegeben von J. M. Lappenberg. 1867.   (*S.R.* Sept. 12.)

*Cracow and Warsaw.   (*S.R.* Oct. 10.)

The late Mr Charles Kean.   (*M.G.* Jan. 28.)

C. Fitzball's "The Prodigal Son," at Prince's Theatre.
(*M.G.* March 3.)

The Life of David Garrick. Review of 'The life of David Garrick,'
by Percy Fitzgerald. 1868.   (*M.G.* March 11.)

Mr Matthew Arnold's "Schools and Universities of the Continent."
Review of 'Schools and Universities of the Continent,' by
Matthew Arnold. 1868.   (*M.G.* March 19.)

Vittoria Colonna. Review of 'Vittoria Colonna: her life and poems,'
by Mrs Henry Roscoe. 1868.   (*M.G.* March 26.)

Oxford University Reorganisation. Review of 'The re-organisation of the University of Oxford,' by Goldwin Smith. 1868.
(*M.G.* April 9.)

"*Hamlet,*" *at Theatre Royal.*   (*M.G.* April 20.)

"*Merchant of Venice,*" *at Theatre Royal.*   (*M.G.* April 28.)

"*Othello,*" *at Theatre Royal.*   (*M.G.* May 1.)

Sheridan Knowles's "*Hunchback*" *and* "*Dr Davy,*" *at Theatre Royal.*
(*M.G.* May 5.)

Madame Birch-Pfeiffer's "*Reinhard and Leonora,*" *at Theatre Royal.*   (*M.G.* May 8.)

Charles Dickens's and Wilkie Collins's "*No Thoroughfare,*" *at Prince's Theatre.*   (*M.G.* May 13.)

Offenbach's "*Grand Duchess of Gerolstein,*" *at Theatre Royal.*
(*M.G.* May 19.)

T. W. Robertson's "*Play,*" *at Prince's Theatre.*   (*M.G.* June 2.)

Shakespeare's "*Comedy of Errors*" *and Victor Hugo's* "*Jean Valjean,*" *at Theatre Royal.*   (*M.G.* June 3.)

Mr Charles Reade's and Mr Dion Boucicault's "*Foul Play,*" *at Theatre Royal.*   (*M.G.* June 24.)

Dion Boucicault's "*Arrah-na-Pogue,*" *at Prince's Theatre.*
(*M.G.* June 25.)

Mr Dickens's farewell readings at Free-Trade Hall.
(*M.G.* Oct. 12.)

"*King Lear,*" *at Prince's Theatre.*   (*M.G.* Oct. 20.)

"*Merry Wives of Windsor,*" *at Theatre Royal.*   (*M.G.* Oct. 20.)

"*Henry IV, Part I,*" *at Prince's Theatre.*   (*M.G.* Oct. 31.)

Leading Article. (Mid-Somerset Election.)   (*M.G.* Nov. 5.)

Henry J. Byron's "Blow for Blow," at Theatre Royal.
                                                    (*M.G.* Nov. 18.)

"Lucrezia Borgia," at Prince's Theatre.   (*M.G.* Nov. 23.)

"Dearer than Life," at Prince's Theatre.   (*M.G.* Dec. 3.)

H. J. Byron's "Not such a Fool as He Looks," at Theatre Royal.
                                                    (*M.G.* Dec. 7.)

Mr Grant Duff's "Political Survey." Review of 'A political survey,' by Mountstuart E. Grant Duff. 1868. (*M.G.* Dec. 16.)

1868–73

The History of Greece. By Ernst Curtius. Translated by A. W. W.
5 vols.

1869

*The House of Austria in the Thirty Years' War. Two Lectures with
notes and illustrations.* (Originally delivered at Edinburgh,
Feb. 3 and 5, 1869.)

Pope's Poetical Works. With notes and introductory memoir, etc.,
by A. W. W. (Globe Edition.) Frequently re-issued.

1870

Charles Dickens. Lecture delivered in Prof. Roscoe's Course of
Science Lectures for the People, at Hulme Town Hall, Manchester, Nov. 30. Manchester.

Von Sybel's "History of the Revolutionary Epoch." Review of:
1. 'Geschichte der Revolutionszeit von 1789 bis 1795,' von
Heinrich von Sybel. Dritte, vermehrte u. verbesserte Aufl.
3 Bde. 1865–6.—2. 'History of the French Revolution,' by
Heinrich von Sybel; translated from the third edition of the

original German work by Walter C. Perry. 4 vols. 1867–70.—
3. 'Oesterreich und Preussen gegenüber der französischen Revolution bis zum Abschluss des Friedens von Campo Formio,' von
Hermann Hüffer. 1868.—4. 'Oesterreich und Deutschland im
Revolutionskrieg. Ergänzungsheft zur Geschichte der Revolutionszeit von 1778 bis 1795,' von Heinrich von Sybel. 1868.—
5. 'Die Politik der deutschen Mächte im Revolutionskriege bis
zum Frieden von Campo Formio,' von Hermann Hüffer. 1869.
—6. 'Polens Untergang und der Revolutionskrieg,' von Heinrich
von Sybel. In *Sybel's Historische Zeitschrift*, Bd. xxiii, Heft 1,
1870.   (*Q.R.* Oct.)

England's Recognition of the Second French Empire.
                               (*Owens College Mag.* Nov.)

Leading Articles on Deaths of Dickens and Lord Clarendon.
                               (*Glasgow Herald*, June.)

Charles Dickens.   (*Glasgow Herald*, July.)

Letters from Brussels, Zurich, Stuttgart, Augsburg, Munich,
Dresden, Leipzig, Berlin and Cologne.
                               (*Glasgow Herald*, July and August.)

Leading Articles on Radical Sympathy with French Republic and
English Neutrality: and plentiful hackwork.
                               (*Glasgow Herald*, Sept.)

Sir Henry Bulwer's "Life of Lord Palmerston." Review of 'Life
of Henry John Temple, Viscount Palmerston,' by Sir Henry
Lytton Bulwer. Vols. i and ii. 1870.
                               (*Glasgow Herald*, Nov.)

Helen Faucit.   (*Glasgow Herald*, Dec.)

What we Demand from France. Translated from H. von Treitschke.
(Parts I and III by W. Jack; part II by A. W. W.) Published
anonymously.

1871

A Catalogue of the Books bequeathed to Owens College, Manchester, by Bishop Lee. Manchester.

A Century of Russian Foreign Policy. Three Lectures delivered at Royal Institution, Manchester, Feb. 13, 20, 27.
(*M.G.* Feb. 14, 21, 28.)

Der Ruhm. (*S.R.* July 8.)

Prison Memoirs of Countess Ulfeldt. Review of 'Denkwürdigkeiten der Gräfin zu Schleswig-Holstein Leonora Christina, vermählten Gräfin Ulfeldt, aus ihrer Gefangenschaft im Blauen Thurm d. Königsschlosses zu Copenhagen, 1663–1685.' Nach der Dän. Original-Handschrift herausgegeben von Johannes Ziegler. 1871. (*S.R.* Nov. 4.)

*Reuchlin. Review of 'Johann Reuchlin, sein Leben und seine Werke,' von Ludwig Geiger. 1871. (*S.R.* Nov. 25.)

Miss Neilson's Juliet. (*M.G.* May 10.)

Palgrave's "Lyrical Poems." Review of 'Lyrical poems,' by Francis Turner Palgrave. 1871. (*M.G.* May 18.)

Miss Helen Faucit's Portia. (*M.G.* Nov.)

Miss Helen Faucit's Rosalind. (*M.G.* Nov. 18.)

"Romeo and Juliet," at Theatre Royal. (*M.G.* Nov. 20.)

"Much Ado About Nothing," at Theatre Royal. (*M.G.* Nov. 24.)

Elwin's "Pope," vol. i. Review of 'The works of Alexander Pope.' New ed., collected in part by J. W. Croker; with introductions and notes, by Whitwell Elwin. Vol. i. 1871.
(*Glasgow Herald*, Jan. 5.)

Leading Article on Engineering College; Notice of Wratislaw's Bohemian Embassy. (*Glasgow Herald*, Feb.)

Elwin's "Pope," vol. II. Review of 'The works of Alexander Pope.' New ed., collected in part by J. W. Croker; with introductions and notes, by Whitwell Elwin. Vol. II. 1871.

(*Glasgow Herald*, Feb. 11.)

Elwin's "Pope," vol. VI (I of Correspondence).

(*Glasgow Herald*, May.)

Elwin's "Pope," vol. VII (II of Correspondence).

(*Glasgow Herald*, June 29.)

Christie's "Life of Shaftesbury." Review of 'A life of Anthony Ashley Cooper, 1st Earl of Shaftesbury, 1621–1683,' by W. D. Christie. 2 vols. 1871.   (*Glasgow Herald*, July 6.)

Forster's "Life of Dickens," vol. I. Review of 'The life of Charles Dickens,' by John Forster. Vol. I. 1871.

(*Glasgow Herald*, Dec. 21.)

Fitzgerald's "Lives of the Kembles." Review of 'The Kembles: an account of the Kemble family,' by Percy Fitzgerald. 2 vols. 1871.   (*Glasgow Herald*, Dec. 23.)

[The Ober-Ammergau Passion-Play. Paper read in Owens College Union, Nov. 24.

Charles Dickens. Lecture delivered at Bolton, Dec. 8.]

1872

Suggestions towards the Establishment of a History Tripos. Cambridge.

*The Study of History at Cambridge.   (*S.R.* July 6.)

Memoirs of Baron von Stockmar. Review of 'Denkwürdigkeiten aus den Papieren des Freiherrn C. F. v. Stockmar'; zusammengestellt von Ernst Fr. v. Stockmar. 1872.   (*S.R.* Aug. 3.)

Friedländer's Roman Manners under the Earlier Emperors, vol. III. Review of 'Darstellungen aus der Sittengeschichte Roms in der Zeit von August bis zum Ausgang der Antonine,' von Ludwig Friedländer. III. Theil. 1871.   (*S.R.* Sept. 7.)

Nichol's "Hannibal." Review of 'Hannibal: a historical drama,' by John Nichol. 1873.   (*S.R.* Nov. 30.)

Songs of Two Worlds. Review of 'Songs of two worlds,' by a new writer (i.e. Lewis Morris). 1871.   (*M.G.* Jan. 11.)

Miss Neilson in "A Life for a Life," at Prince's Theatre.
                                        (*M.G.* May 8.)

Goethe and Mendelssohn.   (*M.G.* June 27.)

Longfellow's "Three Books of Song." Review.   (*M.G.* July 5.)

J. R. Planché's "Recollections and Reflections." Review of 'The recollections and reflections of J. R. Planché.' 2 vols. 1872.
                                        (*M.G.* Aug. 4.)

Blackie's " Lays of the Highlands and Islands." Review of 'Lays of the highlands and islands,' by J. S. Blackie. 1872. (*M.G.* Sept. 6.)

"Henry V." Dramatic Criticism.   (*M.G.* Sept. 18.)

Archbishop Trench's "Gustavus Adolphus," etc. Review of 'Gustavus Adolphus in Germany and other lectures on the Thirty Years' War.' 2nd ed. 1872.   (*Glasgow Herald*, Nov.)

Forster's " Life of Dickens," vol. II. Review of 'The life of Charles Dickens,' by John Forster. Vol. II. 1872.
                                        (*Glasgow Herald*, Nov. 22.)

1873

The Proposed History Tripos. Cambridge.

Ewald's "Life of Algernon Sydney." Review of 'The life and times of the Hon. Algernon Sydney, 1622–1683,' by Alex. Charles Ewald. 2 vols. 1873.   (*S.R.* Feb. 8.)

Free Library Catalogues.   (*S.R.* Feb. 15.)

Picton's "Memorials of Liverpool." Review of 'Memorials of Liverpool; historical and topographical, including a history of the Dock Estate,' by J. A. Picton. 2 vols. 1873.
                                                   (*S.R.* June 21.)

Ingo and Ingraban. Review of 'Die Ahnen, von Gustav Freytag. Erste Abtheilung: Ingo und Ingraban.' 1872.—'Our forefathers, by Gustav Freytag'; translated by Mrs Malcolm. 1873.
                                                   (*S.R.* July 26.)

*Bryce on the New German Empire. Review of 'The Holy Roman Empire,' by James Bryce. 4th ed., with a chapter on the New German Empire 1873.   (*S.R.* Oct. 11.)

Lord Houghton's Monographs. Review of 'Monographs, personal and social,' by Lord Houghton. 1873.   (*M.G.* May 23.)

"Maria Stuart," at Queen's Theatre.   (*M.G.* July 17.)

Outlines of German Literature. Review of 'Outlines of German literature,' by Joseph Gostwick and Robert Harrison. 1873.
                                                   (*M.G.* Oct. 3.)

Literature or Science? The Contencyoun betwene Lettrys and Science.
          (*M.G.* Oct. 9. Reprinted in *Owens Coll. Mag.* Jan. 1874.)

"Midsummer Night's Dream," at Prince's Theatre.
                                                   (*M.G.* Dec. 1.)

Elwin's "Pope," vol. VIII (III of Correspondence).
                                        (*Glasgow Herald*, Jan. 23.)

Tennyson's "Poems." Review.   (*Glasgow Herald*, June 4.)

Freeman's Historical Essays. Second series. Review of 'Historical Essays,' by E. A. Freeman. Second series. 1873.
                                        (*Glasgow Herald*, June 5.)

1874

*The Peace of Europe. Delivered 1873. (Essays and Addresses by professors and lecturers of Owens College, Manchester. Ed. by Balfour Stewart and A. W. W.)

The New Shakespeare Society. (*S.R.* Jan. 3.)

Miss MacArthur's "School History of Scotland." Review of 'History of Scotland,' by Margaret MacArthur. (Vol. III of Historical Course for Schools; edited by E. A. Freeman.) 1873.
(*S.R.* Feb. 14.)

Cox's "History of Greece." Review of 'A history of Greece,' by G. W. Cox. Vols. I and II. 1874. (*S.R.* May 9.)

Cox's "History of Greece." (Second notice.) Review of 'A history of Greece,' by G. W Cox. Vols. I and II. 1874.
(*S.R.* May 16.)

Lancashire Worthies. Review of 'Lancashire worthies,' by Francis Espinasse. 1874. (*S.R.* June 27.)

Mrs Cooper's " Life of Strafford." Review of 'The life of Thomas Wentworth, Earl of Strafford, and Lord-Lieutenant of Ireland,' by Elizabeth Cooper. 2 vols. 1874. (*S.R.* Aug. 1.)

Spedding's "Bacon," vol. VII. Review of 'Letters and life of Francis Bacon,' by James Spedding. Vol. VII. 1874. (*S.R.* Nov. 21.)

Political Articles as to General Election.
(*M.G.* Jan. 29–30, Feb. 1, Feb. 5.)

Mr Bridges's "Poems." Review of 'Poems,' by Robert Bridges. 1873. (*M.G.* Feb. 6.)

Lyrics of the Scots Law. Review of 'Lyrics: legal and miscellaneous,' by George Outram; ed. (with introductory note) by Henry Glassford Bell. 1874. (*M.G.* March 30.)

More about Monaco. Review of 'The fall of Prince Florestan of Monaco,' by himself. 1874. (*M.G.* April 4.)

Poems by George Eliot. Review of 'The legend of Jubal and other poems,' by George Eliot. 1874. (*M.G.* June 19.)

Songs of Two Worlds. Review of 'Songs of two worlds (second series),' by a new writer. 1874. (*M.G.* Dec. 28.)

1875

A History of English Dramatic Literature to the Death of Queen Anne. 2 vols. New edition. 3 vols. 1899.

Types of the Renascence. I. Italy (The Scholar); II. Germany (The Knight); III. Spain (The Monk); IV. England (The Poet). Public Free lectures delivered at Owens College Jan. 25, Feb. 1, 8, 15.   (*M.G.* Jan. 27, Feb. 3, 10, 17.)

Furley's "Weald of Kent," vol. II. Review of 'A history of the Weald of Kent, with an outline of the history of the County to the present time,' by R. Furley. Vol. II. Pts I and II. 1874.
(*S.R.* March 20.)

Gardiner's "England under Buckingham and Charles I." Review of 'A history of England under the Duke of Buckingham and Charles I, 1624–1628,' by Samuel Rawson Gardiner. 2 vols. 1875.   (*S.R.* May 28.)

Sir John Reresby's "Memoirs." Review of 'The memoirs of Sir John Reresby of Thrybergh, Bart., M.P. for York, etc., 1634–1689, written by himself'; edited from the original MS. by James J. Cartwright. 1875.   (*S.R.* July 3.)

The Stair Annals. Review of 'Annals and correspondence of the Viscount and the First and Second Earls of Stair,' by John Murray Graham. 2 vols. 1875.   (*S.R.* Sept. 11.)

Protests of the Lords. Review of 'A complete collection of the Protests of the Lords...,' edited from the journals of the Lords by James E. Thorold Rogers. 3 vols. 1875.   (*S.R.* Oct. 16.)

Mignet's "Charles V and Francis I." Review of 'Rivalité de François Ier et de Charles-Quint,' par M. Mignet. Vols. I and II. 1875.   (*S.R.* Nov. 20.)

Forster's "Life of Swift," vol. I. Review of 'Life of Jonathan Swift,' by John Forster. Vol. I, 1667–1711. 1875.
(*S.R.* Dec. 4.)

Ewald's "*Life of Prince Charles Stuart.*" Review of 'The life and times of Prince Charles Stuart, Count of Albany, commonly called the Young Pretender,' by Alex. Charles Ewald. 2 vols. 1875. (*S.R.* Dec. 18.)

**Hertslet's* "*Map of Europe by Treaty.*" Review of 'The map of Europe by Treaty...,' by E. Hertslet. 3 vols. 1875.
(*S.R.* Dec. 25.)

Mr Calvert's Stage Editions of Shakspere. (*M.G.* April 9.)

G. H. Lewes "*On Actors and the Art of Acting.*" Review of 'On actors and the art of acting,' by George Henry Lewes. 1875.
(*M.G.* Aug. 4.)

"*John Bull,*" *at Theatre Royal.* (*M.G.* Oct. 5.)

"*The School for Scandal,*" *at Theatre Royal.* (*M.G.* Oct. 13.)

Occasional Note. (German Supplementary Penal Code.)
(*M.G.* Oct. 18.)

Occasional Note. (Fugitive Slave Circular.) (*M.G.* Oct. 25.)

**The Stein Monument.* (*M.G.* Oct. 29.)

Occasional Note. (Parliamentary Difficulties of the Reichstag.)
(*M.G.* Nov. 15.)

**Sixty-Nine Years at the Prussian Court.* Review of 'Neunundsechzig Jahre am Preussischen Hofe; aus den Erinnerungen der Oberhofmeisterin Sophie Marie Gräfin von Voss.' 1876.
(*M.G.* Dec. 6.)

Mrs Morgan's Fairy Stories. Review of 'Baron Bruno; or The unbelieving philosopher and other fairy stories,' by Louisa Morgan. 1875. (*M.G.* Dec. 29.)

1876

Pamphlet on the Proposed Conversion of Owens College into a University. (Drawn up at instance and with aid of other members of the Senate.) Manchester.

2–2

Memorandum on Letters in answer to Pamphlet on Proposal to seek for Owens College a University Charter. Manchester.

Memorandum on Newspaper Criticisms of Owens College University Scheme. Manchester.

Four Lectures: Hellenica, or Notes of Greek History and Travel. 1. *Delphi.* 2. *Demos at Home.* 3. *Nauplia and Navarino.* 4. **The University of Athens.* Delivered at Owens College, Nov., Dec. (1 and 3 reported in *M. G.*)

Letters of Sarah Duchess of Marlborough. Review of 'Letters of Sarah, Duchess of Marlborough; now first published from the original MSS. at Madresfield Court.' 1875.   (*S.R.* Jan. 22.)

General Orders of the Duke of Cumberland. Review of 'William Augustus, Duke of Cumberland; being a sketch of his military life and character, chiefly exhibited in the General Orders of H.R.H., 1745–1747,' by Archibald Neil Campbell-Maclachlan. 1876.   (*S.R.* Feb. 12.)

A German View of Junius. Review of 'Die Briefe des Junius,' von Friedrich Brockhaus. 1876.   (*S.R.* March 11.)

Wyon's "Reign of Queen Anne." Review of 'The history of Great Britain during the reign of Queen Anne,' by Frederick William Wyon. 2 vols. 1876.   (*S.R.* April 8.)

The Earls of Middleton. Review of 'The Earls of Middleton, Lords of Clermont and of Fettercairn, and the Middleton Family,' by A. C. Biscoe. 1876.   (*S.R.* April 29.)

Lord Albemarle's Reminiscences. Review of 'Fifty years of my life,' by George Thomas, Earl of Albemarle. 2 vols. 1876.
(*S.R.* May 6.)

Cox's "General History of Greece." Review of 'A general history of Greece from the earliest period to the death of Alexander the Great, with a sketch of the subsequent history to the present time,' by George W. Cox. 1876.   (*S.R.* July 15.)

Stanislas-Augustus and Madame Geoffrin. Review of 'Correspondance inédite du roi Stanislas-August Poniatowski et de Madame Geoffrin (1764–1777). Précédée d'une étude, etc.,' par M. Charles de Mouy.   (*S.R.* Sept. 9.)

The late Dr Cookson.   (*S.R.* Oct. 14.)

James II and the Duke of Berwick. Review of 'James the Second and the Duke of Berwick,' by Charles Townshend Wilson. 1876.
(*S.R.* Nov. 4.)

Cox's "Greeks and Persians," and "Athenian Empire." Review of 'The Greeks and the Persians,' by G. W. Cox.—'The Athenian Empire,' by G. W. Cox. 1876.   (*S.R.* Dec. 9.)

George Eliot's new Novel. Review of 'Daniel Deronda,' by George Eliot. Book I. The spoiled child.   (*M.G.* Jan. 29.)

The late Mr John Forster.   (*M.G.* Feb. 4.)

The Byron Memorial and "Fraser's Magazine." (*M.G.* Feb. 15.)

Victor Hugo on Exile. Review of 'Ce que c'est que l'Exil: introduction au livre Pendant l'Exil,' par Victor Hugo. 1875.
(*M.G.* Feb. 18.)

Daniel Deronda. Book II. Review of 'Daniel Deronda,' by George Eliot. Book II. Meeting streams.   (*M.G.* Feb. 28.)

Signor Salvini in "Othello," at Theatre Royal. (*M.G.* March 15.)

Daniel Deronda. Book IV. Review of 'Daniel Deronda,' by George Eliot. Book IV. Gwendolen gets her choice.
(*M.G.* April 28.)

Mr Julian Hawthorne's Saxon Studies. Review of 'Saxon studies,' by Julian Hawthorne. 1876.   (*M.G.* May 19.)

Daniel Deronda, Book V. Review of 'Daniel Deronda,' by George Eliot. Book V. Mordecai.   (*M.G.* May 30.)

Dion Boucicault's "Rip Van Winkle," at Prince's Theatre.
(*M.G.* May 31.)

Five Letters to the Manchester Guardian from Constantinople, Salonica, and Athens.   (*M.G.* Aug. and Sept.)

Vagrant Verses and a Play. Review of 'Vagrant verses and a play,' by George Staunton Brodie. 1876.   (*M.G.* Nov. 3.)

Madame Chaumont at the Free-Trade Hall.   (*M.G.* Dec. 5.)

1877

Richard Cumberland.   (*Encycl. Brit.* 9th ed. vol. VI.)

Reply to Criticisms of Owens College University Scheme. Manchester.

*Delphi. (Originally delivered as the first of a series of Public Evening Lectures on Greek history and travel at Owens College, Manchester, November 22, 1876.)   (*Cornhill Mag.* July.)

Lecture on the Camisards, to the Owens College Union.
                    (*Owens College Mag.* Dec.)

*Swift's Love-Story in German Literature.
                    (*Macmillan's Mag.* Feb.)

Wyatt's "History of Prussia." Review of 'The history of Prussia, from the earliest times to the present day; tracing the origin and development of her military organization,' by W. J. Wyatt. Vols. I and II. 1876.   (*S.R.* Feb. 3.)

Birchall's "England from 1688 to 1820." Review of 'England under the Revolution and the House of Hanover, 1688–1820,' by James Birchall. 1876.   (*S.R.* March 17.)

The Maid of Stralsund. Review of 'The Maid of Stralsund: a story of the Thirty Years' War,' by J. B. de Liefde.
                    (*S.R.* March 31.)

Curteis's "Rise of the Macedonian Empire." Review of 'Rise of the Macedonian Empire,' by Arthur M. Curteis. (Epochs of Ancient History Series.) 1877.   (*S.R.* April 28.)

Bisset's "Struggle for Parliamentary Government in England."
Review of 'The history of the struggle for Parliamentary
Government in England,' by Andrew Bisset. 2 vols. 1877.
(*S.R.* June 9.)

Abbott's "Bacon and Essex." Review of 'Bacon and Essex: a
sketch of Bacon's earlier life,' by Edwin Abbott. 1877.
(*S.R.* July 7.)

Documents Relating to William Prynne. Review of 'Documents
relating to the proceedings against William Prynne in 1634 and
1637; with a biographical fragment by John Bruce'; edited by
Samuel Rawson Gardiner. 1877.   (*S.R.* July 14.)

Morris's "Age of Anne." Review of 'The age of Anne,' by Edward
E. Morris. (Epochs of Modern History Series.) 1877.
(*S.R.* Aug. 4.)

Lancashire Worthies. Second Series. Review of 'Lancashire
Worthies.' Second series, by Francis Espinasse. 1877.
(*S.R.* Aug. 18.)

Sankey's "Spartan and Theban Supremacies." Review of 'The
Spartan and Theban supremacies,' by Charles Sankey. (Epochs
of Ancient History Series.) 1877.   (*S.R.* Aug. 25.)

Queen Henrietta Maria. Review of 'Henriette-Marie de France,
reine d'Angleterre,' par le Comte de Baillon. 1877.
(*S.R.* Sept. 15.)

Thirty Years After. Review of 'Nach dreissig Jahren.' Neue
Dorfgeschichten von Berthold Auerbach. 3 Bde. 1876.—
'Lorley and Reinhard,' by Berthold Auerbach; translated by
Charles T. Brooks. 1877.—'Aloys the Gawk and Aloys the
American,' by Berthold Auerbach; translated by Charles T.
Brooks. 1877.—'The Convicts and their children,' by
Berthold Auerbach; translated by Charles T. Brooks. 1877.
(*S.R.* Oct. 13.)

Mrs Creighton's " Life of Ralegh." Review of 'Life of Sir Walter Ralegh,' by Louise Creighton. (Historical Biographies 1877.)
(*S.R.* Nov. 24.)

**Gardiner's " Personal Government of Charles I."* Review of 'The personal government of Charles I...1628–1637,' by S. R. Gardiner. 2 vols. 1877.   (*S.R.* Dec. 22.)

Mr Phelps's Farewell Performances. "*Henry VIII*," at Prince's Theatre.   (*M.G.* March 6.)

The Leeuwarden Exhibition. (From an occasional correspondent.)
(*M.G.* Sept. 17.)

Revision of Biographical Introduction to H. Glassford Bell's Edition of Shakespeare. Glasgow.

1878

Drama. (*Encycl. Brit.* 9th ed. vol. VII. Revised for later editions.)

**On Some Academical Experiences of the German Renaissance.* Opening Address at Owens College of Session 1878–9. Published by request of the Council.

Observations on the Leeds Memorial to the Privy Council. Manchester.

Circular in Reference to Leeds Deputation on University Question. Manchester.

Address at Bolton at Distribution of Oxford Local Examination Prizes.
(*Manchester Examiner*, Nov. 7, and *Bolton Chronicle*.)

Bohemian Literature in the Fourteenth Century. Review of 'The native literature of Bohemia in the fourteenth century...,' by A. H. Wratislaw. 1878.   (*Macmillan's Mag.* May.)

**Is it Expedient to Increase the Number of Universities in England?* Paper read at Social Science Congress at Cheltenham, Oct. 25, 1878.   (*Macmillan's Mag.* Nov.)

Doran's " London in the Jacobite Times." Review of 'London in the Jacobite times,' by Dr Doran. 2 vols. 1877.
(*S.R.* Jan. 26.)

Note-Book of Sir John Northcote. Review of 'Note-book of Sir John Northcote, sometime M.P. for Ashburton, and afterwards for the County of Devon, containing memoranda of proceedings in the House of Commons during the first Session of the Long Parliament, 1640; from the MS. original in the possession of the Rt Hon. Sir Stafford Northcote, Bart.' Transcribed and edited, with a memoir, by A. H. A. Hamilton. 1877. (*S.R.* Feb. 9.)

Ewald's " Life of Sir Robert Walpole." Review of 'Sir Robert Walpole: a political biography, 1676–1745,' by Alex. Charles Ewald. 1877.   (*S.R.* March 2.)

Masson's " Life of Milton," vols. IV and V. (First notice.) Review of 'The life of John Milton...,' by David Masson, etc. Vols. IV and V. 1877.   (*S.R.* April 6.)

Masson's " Life of Milton," vols. IV and V. (Second notice.) Review of 'The life of John Milton...,' by David Masson, etc. Vols. IV and V. 1877.   (*S.R.* April 13.)

Lecky's "History of England in the Eighteenth Century." (First notice.) Review of 'A history of England in the Eighteenth Century,' by William Edward Hartpole Lecky. Vols. I and II. 1878.   (*S.R.* May 11.)

Lecky's "History of England in the Eighteenth Century." (Second notice.) Review of 'A history of England in the Eighteenth Century,' by William Edward Hartpole Lecky. Vols. I and II. 1878.   (*S.R.* May 18.)

The Chief Actors in the Puritan Revolution. Review of 'The chief actors in the Puritan Revolution,' by Peter Bayne. 1878.
(*S.R.* July 27.)

The Princess of Eboli. Review of 'La Princesse d'Eboli,' par Gaspar Muro; précédée d'une lettre-préface de M. Canovas del Castillo. Traduit de l'Espagnol par Alfred Weil. 1878. (*S.R.* Aug. 3.)

Historical Ballads of Turco-Graecia. Review of 'Recueil de poëmes historiques en Grec vulgaire relatifs à la Turquie et aux Principautés Danubiennes,' publiés, traduits et annotés par E. Legrand. 1877.   (*S.R.* Aug. 10.)

Payne's "History of European Colonies." Review of 'History of European Colonies,' by Edward J. Payne. (Historical Course for Schools.)   (*S.R.* Oct. 5.)

*Finlay's *"History of Greece."* Review of 'A history of Greece from its conquest by the Romans to the present time,' by George Finlay; ed. by H. F. Tozer. 7 vols.   (*S.R.* Nov. 9.)

Milton's "Poems" for Students. Review of 'The poetical works of John Milton'; ed. with notes, explanatory and philological, by John Bradshaw. 2 vols. 1878.   (*S.R.* Dec. 7.)

Archbishop Trench on the Thirty Years' War; Testament of Peter the Great; Head of the Hansa; Trotter's "Studies in Biography"; Letters to Tieck; Reminiscences of the Weimar Stage; were sent to the *Saturday Review,* but never inserted.

Lady Charlotte Elliot's "Poems." Review of 'Medusa and other poems,' by Lady Charlotte Elliot. 1878.   (*M.G.* April 22.)

The late Mr Phelps.   (*M.G.* Nov. 8.)

Count Arnim's "The Nuncio is Coming." (Article.)
                                        (*M.G.* Nov. 20.)

Old English Drama. Select Plays. Marlowe's "Tragical History of Doctor Faustus" and Greene's "Honourable History of Friar Bacon and Friar Bungay." Edited by A. W. W. 1878.

1879

Samuel Foote.   (*Encycl. Brit.* 9th ed. vol. IX.)

John Ford.   (*Encycl. Brit.* 9th ed. vol. IX.)

David Garrick. (R. Carruthers revised.)
                                        (*Encycl. Brit.* 9th ed. vol. X.)

Memorials, Report to Court, etc., on University Question. Manchester.

Court Report on University Question. Manchester.

Reaction and Decline. Lecture at the College for Women, Brunswick Street, Oct. 21.   (*M.G.* Oct. 22.)

Pi-Pa-Ki.   (*Owens College Mag.* June.)

Robert Greene. Paper at Owens College Shakspere Society.
                              (*Owens College Mag.* Dec.)

Mrs Potter's "Lancashire Memories." Review of 'Lancashire memories,' by Louisa Potter. 1879. (*Manchester Mag.* Sept.)

Tennyson's "Lover's Tale."—Browning's "Dramatic Idylls." Review of 1. 'The lover's tale,' by Alfred Tennyson. 1879.— 2. 'Dramatic idylls,' by Robert Browning. 1879.
                              (*Deutsches Literaturbl.* Aug. 1.)

George Eliot's "Impressions of Theophrastus Such" (1). Review of 'Impressions of Theophrastus Such,' by G. Eliot. 1879.
                              (*Deutsches Literaturbl.* Sept. 15.)

George Eliot's "Impressions of Theophrastus Such" (2). Review of 'Impressions of Theophrastus Such,' by G. Eliot. 1879.
                              (*Deutsches Literaturbl.* Oct. 1.)

Memoir of Catharine & Craufurd Tait. Review of 'Catharine and Craufurd Tait: a memoir,' by William Benham. 1879.
                              (*Deutsches Literaturbl.* Nov.)

The Hatton Correspondence. Review of 'Correspondence of the family of Hatton, being chiefly letters addressed to Christopher, First Viscount Hatton, A.D. 1601–1704'; ed. by Edward Maunde Thompson. 2 vols. Printed for the Camden Society. 1878.   (*S.R.* March 15.)

Blue and Green. Review of 'Blue and green; or The gift of God, a romance of old Constantinople,' by Sir Henry Pottinger. 3 vols.   (*S.R.* April 5.)

Quarter Sessions from Elizabeth to Anne. Review of 'Quarter sessions from Queen Elizabeth to Queen Anne...,' by A. H. A. Hamilton. 1878.   (*S.R.* May 10.)

Froude's "Caesar." Review of 'Caesar: a sketch,' by James Anthony Froude. 1879.   (*S.R.* May 31.)

The Tudors Re-painted. Review of 'Historical portraits of the Tudor dynasty and the Reformation period,' by S. Hubert Burke. Vol. I. 1879.   (*S.R.* June 21.)

Treitschke's "German History." Review of 'Deutsche Geschichte im 19. Jahrhundert.' I. Theil. (Staaten-Geschichte der neuesten Zeit.) 1879.   (*S.R.* July 5.)

Oscar II on Charles XII. Review of 'Charles XII,' by "Oscar Fredrik"; translated from the original Swedish by George F. Apgeorge. 1879.   (*S.R.* Aug. 9.)

The Pythouse Papers. Review of 'The Pythouse papers: correspondence concerning the Civil War, the Popish plot and a contested election in 1680.' Transcribed from a MS. in the possession of V. F. Benett-Stanford; ed., and with an introduction, by William Ansell Day. 1879.   (*S.R.* Oct. 4.)

Representative Statesmen. Review of 'Representative Statesmen: political studies,' by A. C. Ewald. 2 vols. 1879.
                                        (*S.R.* Nov. 15.)

Germany, Present and Past. Review of 'Germany, present and past,' by S. Baring-Gould. 2 vols. 1879.   (*S.R.* Nov. 29.)

Pascoe's "Dramatic Register." Review of 'The dramatic list'; ed. by C. E. Pascoe. 1879.   (*M.G.* March 31.)

Review of 'The life of Charles James Mathews, chiefly autobiographical, with selections from his correspondence'; ed. by Charles Dickens. 2 vols. 1879.   (*M.G.* Aug. 18.)

Calvert memorial performance, at Theatre Royal. The late Charles Calvert.   (*M.G.* Oct. 2.)

Treitschke and the Jews in Germany.   (*M.G.* Dec.)

The Letters of Charles Dickens. Review of 'The letters of Charles
   Dickens'; ed. by his sister-in-law and his eldest daughter. 2 vols.
   1880.   (*M.G.* Dec. 15.)

[Lecture on Charles Dickens. (Revised.) Burnley, Dec. 11.]

1880

Chaucer. (English Men of Letters Series.)

Robert Greene.   (*Encycl. Brit.* 9th ed. vol. xi.)

The Fleet Prison in the Seventeenth Century. Review of 'The
   Œconomy of the Fleete: or, An Apologeticall Answeare of
   Alexander Harris (late Warden there) into XIX. Articles sett
   forth against him by the Prisoners'; edited by Augustus Jessopp.
   Printed for the Camden Society. 1879.   (*S.R.* Jan. 10.)

*Pattison's "Milton." Review of 'Milton,' by Mark Pattison.
   (English Men of Letters Series.) 1879.   (*S.R.* Feb. 7.)

The Administration of John de Witt. Review of 'History of the
   administration of John de Witt, Grand Pensionary of Holland,'
   by James Geddes. Vol. i. 1623–1654. 1879. (*S.R.* Feb. 28.)

*Rheinsberg. Review of 'Rheinsberg: memorials of Frederick the
   Great and Prince Henry of Prussia,' by Andrew Hamilton.
   2 vols. 1880.   (*S.R.* March 13.)

Masson's "Life of Milton," vol. vi. Review of 'The life of John
   Milton...,' by David Masson. Vol. vi. 1660–1674. 1880.
                                                (*S.R.* March 20.)

Burton's "Reign of Queen Anne." (First notice.) Review of 'A
   history of the reign of Queen Anne,' by John Hill Burton.
   3 vols. 1880.   (*S.R.* April 10.)

Burton's "Reign of Queen Anne." (Second notice.) Review of 'A history of the reign of Queen Anne,' by John Hill Burton. 3 vols. 1880. (*S.R.* April 24.)

The Religious Drama. Review of 'Miracle plays and sacred dramas; a historical survey,' by Karl Hase. Translated from the German by A. W. Jackson, and ed. by W. W. Jackson. 1880.
(*S.R.* May 1.)

Memorials of Huguenot Persecution. Review of 'Deux héroïnes de la Foi: Blanche Gamond, Jeanne Terrason...,' publiés par Th. Claparède et Ed. Goby. 1880.—'La Tour de Constance et ses prisonnières. Liste générale et documents inédits,' par Charles Sagnier. 1880. (*S.R.* June 19.)

Leslie Stephen on Pope. Review of 'Alexander Pope,' by Leslie Stephen. (English Men of Letters Series.) 1880.
(*S.R.* July 10.)

A Cavalier's Note-Book. Review of 'Crosby Records; a cavalier's note-book: being notes, anecdotes and observations of William Blundell of Crosby, Lancashire.' Edited, with introductory chapters, by T. Ellison Gibson. 1880. (*S.R.* July 17.)

Hillebrand on Modern German Thought. Review of 'Six lectures on the history of German thought from the Seven Years' War to Goethe's death...,' by Karl Hillebrand. 1880. (*S.R.* Oct. 9.)

Anecdotes of Parliament. Review of 'An anecdotal history of the British parliament from the earliest period to the present time'; compiled from authentic sources, by George Henry Jennings. 1880. (*S.R.* Nov. 13.)

Burke's "Historical Portraits." Review of 'Historical portraits of the Tudor dynasty and the Reformation period,' by S. Hubert Burke. Vol. II. 1880. (*S.R.* Dec. 4.)

Étienne Dolet. Review of 'Étienne Dolet, the martyr of the Renaissance; a biography,' by Richard Copley Christie. 1880.
(*S.R.* Dec. 25.)

Treitschke and Grätz on the Jews in Germany. (*M.G.* Jan. 3.)

Ben Jonson, Cartwright, Oldham, *Dryden, in "*The English Poets*," edited by T. H. Ward, vol. II.

1880–81

Franz Atterbury.—Franz Bacon. (*Herbst's Encyklopädie der neueren Geschichte*, Bd. I.) Gotha.

Benjamin Disraeli, Earl of Beaconsfield. (*Herbst's Encyklopädie der neueren Geschichte*, Bd. I.) Gotha.

Henry St John, Viscount Bolingbroke. (*Herbst's Encyklopädie der neueren Geschichte*, Bd. I.) Gotha.

Edmund Burke. (*Herbst's Encyklopädie der neueren Geschichte*, Bd. I.) Gotha.

John Stuart, Earl of Bute. (*Herbst's Encyklopädie der neueren Geschichte*, Bd. I.) Gotha.

1881

Hrosvitha. (Frequently Roswitha and properly Hrolsuit.)
(*Encycl. Brit.* 9th ed. vol. XII.)

Don John of Austria.—Ben Jonson.
(*Encycl. Brit.* 9th ed. vol. XIII.)

Trollope's "Life of Cicero." Review of 'The life of Cicero,' by Anthony Trollope. 2 vols. 1880.   (*S.R.* Feb. 26.)

The Hamilton Papers. Review of 'The Hamilton Papers; being selections from original letters in the possession of His Grace the Duke of Hamilton and Brandon, relating to the years 1638–1650.' Ed. by S. R. Gardiner. Printed for the Camden Society. 1880.
(*S.R.* March 26.)

Saintsbury's "Dryden." Review of 'Dryden,' by G. Saintsbury. (English Men of Letters Series.) 1881.   (*S.R.* April 2.)

Forneron's "History of Philip II." Review of 'Histoire de Philippe II,' par H. F. Forneron. Tomes I et II. 1881.
(*S.R.* April 30.)

Calendar of State Papers, Domestic Series, 1640. Review of 'Calendar of State Papers, Domestic Series, of the reign of Charles I, 1640,' edited by W. D. Hamilton. 1880.

(*S.R.* July 23.)

The Haigs of Bemersyde. Review of 'The Haigs of Bemersyde: a family history,' by John Russell. 1881.   (*S.R.* Oct. 29.)

Calendar of State Papers, Domestic Series, 1654. Review of 'Calendar of State Papers, Domestic Series, 1654,' edited by Mary Anne Everett Green. 1880.   (*S.R.* Nov. 5.)

[The Ship of Fools. Lecture delivered at Ilkley, Feb. 25.

Address at banquet to Mr Henry Irving in Manchester.]

1882

Dickens. (English Men of Letters Series.)

Thomas Lodge.   (*Encycl. Brit.* 9th ed. vol. xiv.)

*The Brethren of Deventer.   (*Cornhill Mag.* Aug.)

Patriotic Poetry.   (*Macmillan's Mag.* Oct.)

Ewald's "Stories from the State Papers." Review of 'Stories from the State Papers,' by Alex. Charles Ewald. 2 vols. 1882.

(*S.R.* Jan. 28.)

*Gardiner's "Fall of the Monarchy of Charles I." (First notice.) Review of 'The Fall of the Monarchy of Charles I.—1637–1649,' by Samuel Rawson Gardiner. Vols. I and II.—1637–1642. 1882.   (*S.R.* April 8.)

The House of Waldeck.   (*S.R.* April 22.)

*Gardiner's "Fall of the Monarchy of Charles I." (Second notice.) Review of 'The Fall of the Monarchy of Charles I.—1637–1649,' by Samuel Rawson Gardiner. Vols. I and II.—1637–1642. 1882   (*S.R.* April 29.)

Mr William Bodham Donne. (*S.R.* July 1.)

Lecky's "History of England in the Eighteenth Century," vols. III and IV. Review of 'A history of England in the Eighteenth Century,' by William Edward Hartpole Lecky. Vols. III and IV. 1882. (*S.R.* July 15.)

State Papers, Domestic Series, 1655. Review of 'Calendar of State Papers, Domestic Series, 1655'; ed. by Mary Anne Everett Green. 1881. (*S.R.* July 22.)

Three Fifteenth-Century Chronicles. Review of 'Three Fifteenth-century chronicles, with historical memoranda by John Stowe, the antiquary, and contemporary notes of occurrences written by him in the reign of Queen Elizabeth'; ed. by James Gairdner. Printed for the Camden Society. (*S.R.* Aug. 19.)

Ancient Battle-fields in Lancashire. Review of 'On some ancient battle-fields in Lancashire and their historical, legendary and aesthetic associations,' by Charles Hardwick. 1882.
(*S.R.* Nov. 11.)

The Princess of Ahlden. (*S.R.* Nov. 11.)

German Literature made Easy. Review of 'Student's manual of German literature,' by E. Nicholson. (*S.R.* Dec. 2.)

The late Professor W. S. Jevons. (Letter to *M.G.* Aug. 19.)

Creighton's "History of the Papacy During the Reformation." Review of 'A history of the Papacy during the period of the Reformation,' by M. Creighton. Vols. I and II. 1882.
(*M.G.* Dec. 6.)

1883

Grossbritannien. (*Herbst's Encyklopädie der neueren Geschichte,* Bd. II.) Gotha.

The English Renascence. Lecture at Manchester Grammar School, Oct. 18. (*M.G.* Oct. 19.)

Le Théâtre sous la Révolution.   (*Owens College Mag.* April.)

The Wentworth Papers. Review of 'The Wentworth Papers, 1705–1739; selected from the private and family correspondence of Thomas Wentworth, Lord Raby, created in 1711, Earl of Strafford'; with a memoir and notes by James J. Cartwright. 1883.   (*S.R.* Jan. 20.)

Treitschke's "German History," vol. II. Review of 'Deutsche Geschichte im neunzehnten Jahrhundert,' von Heinrich von Treitschke. II. Theil. (Vol. xxv of Staatengeschichte der neuesten Zeit.) 1882.   (*S.R.* Feb. 17.)

James and Philip van Arteveld. Review of 'James and Philip van Arteveld: two episodes in the history of the fourteenth century,' by James Hutton. 1882.   (*S.R.* March 3.)

Calendar of State Papers, Domestic Series, 1640–1641. Review of 'Calendar of State Papers, Domestic Series, of the reign of Charles I, 1640–1641,' ed. by W. D. Hamilton. 1882.
        (*S.R.* March 17.)

Burke's "Tudor Portraits," vol. III. Review of 'Historical portraits of the Tudor dynasty and the Reformation period,' by S. Hubert Burke. Vol. III. 1883.   (*S.R.* April 7.)

*The New Tripos.   (*S.R.* May 5.)

Life of Sir William Rowan Hamilton, vol. I. Review of 'Life of Sir William Rowan Hamilton, including selections from his poems, correspondence and miscellaneous writings,' by Robert Percival Graves. Vol. I. (Dublin University Press Series.) 1882.
        (*S.R.* June 16.)

Calendar of Treasury Papers, 1714–1719. Review of 'Calendar of Treasury Papers, 1714–1719, preserved in the Public Record Office'; prepared by Joseph Redington. 1883. (*S.R.* Sept. 23.)

Gardiner's "History of England." Review of 'History of England from the accession of James I to the outbreak of the Civil War, 1603–1642,' by Samuel R. Gardiner. 10 vols. Vols. I to III. 1883.   (*S.R.* Oct. 13.)

Liverpool Municipal Records. Review of 'City of Liverpool: selections from the municipal archives and records from the 13th to the 17th century inclusive'; extracted and annotated by Sir James A. Picton. 1883.   (*S.R.* Nov. 24.)

Nichol's "American Literature." Review of 'American literature: an historical sketch, 1620–1880,' by John Nichol.
(*M.G.* Feb. 7.)

Saintsbury's "Short History of French Literature." Review of 'A short history of French literature,' by George Saintsbury. 1882.
(*M.G.* March 14.)

John Dryden. Review of 'The works of John Dryden, with notes and life by Sir Walter Scott'; revised and corrected by George Saintsbury. Vols. I and II.   (*M.G.* June 29.)

Review of 'Saintsbury's Specimens of French Literature.'
(*M.G.* Aug.)

Light Luther Literature. Review of 'Martin Luther, the reformer,' by Julius Koestlin; translated from the German by Elizabeth P. Weir.—'Luther: a short biography,' by James Anthony Froude. —'Luther anecdotes: memorable sayings and doings of Martin Luther,' by Dr Macaulay.   (*M.G.* Nov. 12.)

Saintsbury's "Dryden." Review of 'The works of John Dryden.' Sir Walter Scott's edition. Revised and corrected by George Saintsbury. Vols. III and IV.   (*M.G.* Nov. 28.)

Italian Byways. Review of 'Italian byways,' by John Addington Symonds.   (*M.G.* Dec. 6.)

Hostilities without Declaration of War.
(Leading Article, *M.G.* Dec. 24.)

[Confessions of a Critic. Paper read at Owens College Union, Jan. 26.]

1884

Alexander Alesius. (*D.N.B.* vol. i.)

Queen Anne. (*D.N.B.* vol. i.)

Anne of Denmark. (*D.N.B.* vol. i.)

Lancashire Gleanings. Review of 'Lancashire gleanings,' by William E. A. Axon. (*S.R.* March 15.)

Historical Portraits of the Tudor Period, vol. iv. Review of 'Historical portraits of the Tudor dynasty and the Reformation period,' by S. Hubert Burke. Vol. iv. (*S.R.* March 22.)

The Duke of Berwick. Review of 'The Duke of Berwick, Marshal of France—1702–1734,' by Charles Townshend Wilson. (*S.R.* March 29.)

Don John of Austria. Review of 'Don John of Austria; or passages from the history of the sixteenth century, 1547–1578,' by Sir William Stirling-Maxwell, Bart. 2 vols. (*S.R.* May 17.)

Gardiner's "History of England." Review of 'History of England from the accession of James I to the outbreak of the Civil War, 1603–1642,' by Samuel R. Gardiner. 10 vols. Vols. iii–vi. 1883–4. (*S.R.* May 24.)

Calendar of State Papers, Domestic Series, 1656–1657. Review of 'Calendar of State Papers, Domestic Series, 1656–1657'; ed. by Mary Anne Everett Green. 1883. (*S.R.* June 21.)

Southampton. Review of 'A history of Southampton; partly from the MS. of Dr Speed in the Southampton archives,' by J. Silvester Davies. (*S.R.* Aug. 30.)

Gardiner's "History of England," vols. vii–x. Review of 'History of England from the accession of James I to the outbreak of the Civil War, 1603–1642,' by Samuel R. Gardiner. Vols. vii–x. 1884. (*S.R.* Oct. 4.)

Vico. Review of 'Vico,' by Robert Flint. (Philosophical Classics for English Readers.) 1884.   (*S.R.* Nov. 29.)

The Peterhouse Sexcentenary.   (*S.R.* Dec. 20.)

*Duentzer's "Life of Goethe." Review of 'Life of Goethe,' by Heinrich Duentzer; translated by Thomas W. Lyster. 2 vols.   (*M.G.* Jan. 5.)

The Bismarck-Lasker Incident.   (Short Leader, *M.G.* March 7.)

Memoirs of the Earl of Malmesbury. Review of 'Memoirs of an Ex-Minister: an autobiography,' by the Rt Hon. the Earl of Malmesbury. 2 vols.   (*M.G.* Oct. 15.)

1885

Hugh de Balsham.   (*D.N.B.* vol. III.)

Alexander Barclay.   (*D.N.B.* vol. III.)

William Bentinck, First Earl of Portland.   (*D.N.B.* vol. IV.)

Pantomime.   (*Encycl. Brit.* 9th ed. vol. XVIII.)

Elizabeth of Bohemia. Lecture delivered to Bowdon Literary and Scientific Institute, Feb. 24.
    (Pr. in *Coll. Papers*, vol. I, 1921.)

Edmund Roscoe. Obituary Notice.   (*Owens College Mag.* March.)

The Electress Sophia. Review of 1. 'Memoiren der Herzogin Sophie, nachmals Kurfürstin von Hannover.' Herausgegeben von Adolf Köcher. 1879. (Publicationen aus den K. Preuss. Staatsarchiven, Bd. IV.)—2. 'Correspondance de Leibniz avec l'électrice Sophie de Brunswick-Lunebourg.' 3 tomes. 1874.— 3. 'Briefe der Herzogin von Orleans, Elisabeth Charlotte, an die Kurfürstin Sophie von Hannover.' (Ranke, *Französische Geschichte*, Bd. V.)—4. 'Briefe der Prinzessin Elisabeth Charlotte von Orleans, 1676–1722.' (Bibliothek des literarischen Vereins zu Stuttgart, Bd. VI.)—5. 'Geschichte der Lande Braunschweig und Lüneburg,' von W. Havemann. 3 Bde. 1857.—

6. 'Geschichte von Hannover und Braunschweig, 1648 bis 1714,' von A. Köcher. Theil I. 1884. (Publicationen aus den K. Preuss. Staatsarchiven, Bd. xx.)—7. 'Geschichte der rhein-ischen Pfalz,' von L. Häusser. 2te Aus. 2 Bde. 1856.—8. 'Die Herzogin von Ahlden, Stammutter der Königlichen Häuser Hannover und Preussen.' 1852.—9. 'Sophia Dorothea, Prin-zessin von Ahlden, und Kurfürstin Sophie von Hannover.' 1879. —10. 'Die Prinzessin von Ahlden,' von A. Köcher. (In *Sybel's Historische Zeitschrift*, Bd. xlviii.) 1882.   (*Q.R.* July.)

Wiclif.   (*Harper's Mag.* Jan.)

Review of 'The University of Cambridge from the Royal injunc-tions of 1535 to the accession of Charles the First,' by James Bass Mullinger.   (*Academy*, Jan. 10.)

A Dictionary of English History. Review of 'The dictionary of English history'; ed. by Sidney J. Low and F. S. Pulling. 1884.
       (*S.R.* Feb. 14.)

Calendar of State Papers, Colonial Series, 1625–1629. Review of 'Calendar of State Papers, Colonial Series—East Indies, China, and Persia, 1625–1629'; ed. by W. Noel Sainsbury. 1884.
       (*S.R.* March 7.)

Saintsbury's "Dryden," vols. ix and x. Review of 'The works of John Dryden; illustrated with notes, historical, critical and explanatory, and a life of the author, by Sir Walter Scott; revised and corrected by George Saintsbury.' Vols. ix and x. 1884–5.
       (*S.R.* March 28.)

Calendar of State Papers, Domestic Series, 1657–1658. Review of 'Calendar of State Papers, Domestic Series, 1657–1658'; ed. by Mary Anne Everett Green. 1884.   (*S.R.* May 9.)

Calendar of State Papers, Venetian Series, 1557–1558. Review of 'Calendar of State Papers and Manuscripts, relating to English affairs, existing in the Archives of Venice and in other libraries in northern Italy; with an appendix'; ed. by Rawdon Brown. Vol. vi, Part iii, 1557–1558.   (*S.R.* July 4.)

*Köcher's "History of Hanover and Brunswick." Review of 'Geschichte von Hannover und Braunschweig, 1648 bis 1714,' von Adolf Köcher. 1. Theil (1648–1668). (Publ. aus den K. Preuss. Staatsarchiven.) 1884.   (*S.R.* Oct. 24.)

From Shakespeare to Pope. Review of 'From Shakespeare to Pope: an inquiry into the causes and phenomena of the rise of classical poetry in England,' by Edmund Gosse. 1885. (*S.R.* Dec. 12.)

1886

Richard Brome.	(*D.N.B.* vol. VI.)
Martin Bucer.	(*D.N.B.* vol. VII.)
James Butler, 2nd Duke of Ormonde.	(*D.N.B.* vol. VIII.)
James Butler, d. 1634.	(*D.N.B.* vol. VIII.)
Walter, Count Butler.	(*D.N.B.* vol. VIII.)
Charles Alexander Calvert.	(*D.N.B.* vol. VIII.)
Caroline, Queen of George II.	(*D.N.B.* vol. IX.)
Caroline Matilda, Queen of Denmark and Norway.	(*D.N.B.* vol. IX.)

Karl Ritter. Address to the Manchester Geographical Society at the Exhibition of Geographical Appliances, April 9.
        (*M.G.* April 10. *Journal of Manchester Geog. Soc.* June.)

A Goethe Society for Manchester: A Manchester Branch of the Goethe Society. Address to a preliminary meeting at Owens College, April 16.   (*M.G.* April 19.)

Address on Laying of Foundation Stone of the Simpson Memorial Institute at Moston, near Manchester, Aug. 14.
                    (*M.G.* Aug. 16.)

Address at Burnley Grammar School, at Distribution of Prizes, October 14.   (*M.G.* Oct. 15.)

Address at Opening of Manchester Goethe Society in the Manchester Schiller-Anstalt, Oct. 23.   (*M.G.* Oct. 25.)

Memoirs of Mary II. Review of 'Memoirs of Mary, Queen of England (1689–1693), together with her letters, and those of Kings James II and William III to the Electress Sophia of Hanover'; ed. by R. Doebner. 1886. (*Edinburgh Rev.* April.)

Review of 'The official Baronage of England, showing the succession, dignities and offices of every peer from 1066 to 1885,' by James E. Doyle. Vols. I–III. 1886.   (*E.H.R.* April.)

Review of 'Berlin und Wien in den Jahren 1845–1852. Politische Privatbriefe des damaligen K. Sächsischen Legations-Secretärs Karl Friedrich, Grafen Vitzthum von Eckstädt'; mit einem Vorworte von Dr Karl Müller. 1886.   (*E.H.R.* April.)

Review of 'Zeitschrift des historischen Vereins für Niedersachsen.' 1885.   (*E.H.R.* April.)

The Electress Sophia and the Hanoverian Succession. (*E.H.R.* July.)

Review of 'Deutsche Geschichte im neunzehnten Jahrhundert,' von Heinrich von Treitschke. Bd. III. 1885.   (*E.H.R.* Oct.)

Note on Death of Professor Waitz.   (*E.H.R.* Oct.)

Note on Kuno Fischer's Speech at Heidelberg Jubilee.

(*E.H.R.* Oct.)

Saintsbury's "Dryden," vols. XI and XII. Review of 'The works of John Dryden; with notes and life by Sir Walter Scott, revised and corrected by George Saintsbury.' Vols. XI and XII.

(*S.R.* Jan. 23.)

Memoirs of Colonel Hutchinson. Review of 'Memoirs of the life of Colonel Hutchinson, Governor of Nottingham, by his widow Lucy'; ed. by Julius Hutchinson. Revised, with additional notes by C. H. Firth.   (*S.R.* March 6.)

Calendar of State Papers, Domestic Series, 1658–1659. Review of 'Calendar of State Papers, Domestic Series, 1658–1659'; ed. by Mary Anne Everett Green. 1886.   (*S.R.* May 15.)

Baumgarten's "Charles V." Review of 'Geschichte Karls V.,' von Hermann Baumgarten. I. Bd.   (*S.R.* July 31.)

Letters and Journals of W. S. Jevons. Review of 'Letters and Journals of W. Stanley Jevons'; ed. by his wife. 1886.
(S.R. Aug. 28.)

Diary and Letters of Thomas Hutchinson, vol. II. Review of 'The diary and letters of his Excellency Thomas Hutchinson; compiled from the original documents still remaining in the possession of his descendants,' by Peter Orlando Hutchinson. Vol. II. 1886.
(S.R. Sept. 25.)

Admiral Blake. Review of 'Admiral Blake,' by David Hannay. (English Worthies Series.) 1886.
(S.R. Oct. 30.)

Part of Leading Article on Greek Question.   (*M.G.* March 3.)

Seeley's "Short History of Napoleon." Review of 'A short history of Napoleon the First,' by J. R. Seeley. 1886.
(M.G. March 3.)

[Address at Distribution of Prizes at Bury High School for Girls, Nov. 12.]

1887

Charles II, King of England   (*D.N.B.* vol. x.)

Charlotte Augusta Matilda, Queen of Würtemberg.
(D.N.B. vol. x.)

Henry Wilkinson Cookson.   (*D.N.B.* vol. XII.)

The Parnassus Plays. Address to Owens College Shakespeare Society and Union, March 19.   (*M.G.* March 21.)

Address to Manchester Goethe Society, Oct. 22.   (*M.G.* Oct. 24.)

The Victoria University. Conferment of degrees. Vice-Chancellor's Annual Statement, Nov. 3.
(M.G. Nov. 4.)

The Citadel of the German Knights. Address to the Lancashire and Cheshire Antiquarian Society, Dec. 16.
(Trans. L. and C. Ant. Soc.)

Review of 'Die armirten Stände und die Reichskriegsverfassung (1681–1687),' von Richard Fester. 1886.   (*E.H.R.* Jan.)

Review of 'The methods of historical study: eight lectures read in the University of Oxford in Michaelmas Term, 1884,—with the inaugural lecture on the Office of the Historical Professor,' by Edward A. Freeman. 1886.   (*E.H.R.* April.)

Review of 'History of the Great Civil War, 1642–1649,' by S. R. Gardiner. Vol. I, 1642–1644. 1886.   (*E.H.R.* April.)

Review of 'Geschichte Karls V.,' von Hermann Baumgarten. Bd. II; Hälfte I. 1886.   (*E.H.R.* July.)

Review of 'St Petersburg und London in den Jahren 1852–1864; aus den Denkwürdigkeiten von Carl Friedrich Graf Vitzthum von Eckstädt.' 2 Bde. 1886.—'St Petersburg and London in the years 1852–1864; reminiscences of Count Charles Frederick Vitzthum von Eckstaedt, late Saxon Minister at the Court of St James'; ed., with a preface, by Henry Reeve, translated by Edward Fairfax Taylor. 2 vols. 1887.   (*E.H.R.* July.)

Review of 'Old Herbert Papers at Powis Castle and in the British Museum.' Extra vol. (vol. xx) of the collections, historical and archaeological relating to Montgomeryshire and its borders. Issued by the Powysland Club. Privately printed. 1886.
                                                (*E.H.R.* Oct.)

The Parnassus Plays.   (*Owens College Mag.* July.)

Symonds's "Renaissance in Italy," vols. VI and VII. Review of 'Renaissance in Italy—The Catholic reaction,' by John Addington Symonds. 2 pts.   (*S.R.* March 5.)

The Owens College, Manchester. Review of 'The Owens College; its foundation and growth, and its connexion with the Victoria University, Manchester,' by Joseph Thompson.
                                                (*S.R.* March 26.)

Baird's "Huguenots and Henry of Navarre." Review of 'The Huguenots and Henry of Navarre.' 2 vols.   (*S.R.* April 30.)

Creighton's "History of the Papacy," vols. III and IV. Review of 'A history of the Papacy during the period of the Reformation,' by M. Creighton. Vols. III and IV.—The Italian Princes, 1464–1518. 1887.   (*S.R.* June 4.)

Lecky's "History of England in the Eighteenth Century," vols. V and VI. Review of 'A history of England in the Eighteenth Century,' by William Edward Hartpole Lecky. Vols. V and VI. 1887.
                                                    (*S.R.* June 18.)

Manchester. Review of 'Manchester,' by George Saintsbury. 1887.
                                                    (*S.R.* July 16.)

Queen Anne and her Court.   (*S.R.* Oct. 22.)

Review of 'Exeter,' by Edward A. Freeman. (Historic Towns Series.)   (*M.G.* April 8.)

Review of 'The historical basis of modern Europe (1760–1815),' by Archibald Weir.   (*M.G.* April 8.)

Review of 'Rambles and studies in Greece,' by J. P. Mahaffy. 3rd ed.   (*M.G.* April 11.)

Review of 'A history of the Papacy during the period of the Reformation,' by M. Creighton. Vols. III and IV.—The Italian Princes, 1464–1518.   (*M.G.* May 2.)

Mr Lecky's new volumes. Review of 'A history of England in the Eighteenth Century,' by William Edward Hartpole Lecky. Vols. V and VI.   (*M.G.* June 3.)

Review of 'The works of John Dryden; with notes, etc., by Sir Walter Scott.' Revised and corrected by George Saintsbury. Vol. XIII.   (*M.G.* Nov. 7.)

Short Leader on the late Professor Balfour Stewart.
                                                    (*M.G.* Dec. 20.)

Old English Drama. 2nd ed. Revised. Oxford.

[Address at Annual Meeting of Fallowfield and Ladybarn Club, Jan. 28.

Victoria University Application for a public grant. Statement to Chancellor of Exchequer (Mr Goschen) at deputation from Victoria University, March 11.]

1888

William Craven, Earl of Craven, 1606–1697. (*D.N.B.* vol. XIII.)

Address to the Annual Meeting of the Ancoats Art Museum, June 11.
(*M.G.* June 12.)

Address at the Annual Prize Distribution of the Manchester Diocesan Board of Education, June 16.   (*M.G.* June 18.)

Address at Trauerfeier for the Emperor Frederick in Manchester Concert Hall, June 22.   (*M.G.* June 23.)

**The Turrettini Family of Geneva.* Review of 'Notice biographique sur Bénédict Turrettini, Théologien Genevois du XVIIᵉ siècle; d'après des matériaux historiques et des documents rassemblés et mis en ordre par François Turrettini.' (Privately pr.) 1871.
(*Edinburgh Rev.* Oct.)

Review of 'Zur Geschichte Deutschlands und Frankreichs im neunzehnten Jahrhundert,' von Leopold von Ranke; herausgegeben von Alfred Dove. 1887.   (*E.H.R.* Jan.)

Was Anne of Denmark a Catholic? Review of 'Er Frederik II's Datter Anna, Dronning af Storbritannien, gaaet over til Katholicismen?' By W. Plenkers. 1888.   (*E.H.R.* Oct.)

The Pope Commemoration.   (*Owens College Mag.* Oct.)

Calendar of State Papers, Domestic Series, 1641–1643. Review of 'Calendar of State Papers, Domestic Series, of the reign of Charles I, 1641–1643'; ed. by W. D. Hamilton.
(*S.R.* June 16.)

Tuttle's "Prussia under Frederick the Great." Review of 'History of Prussia under Frederick the Great, 1740–1756,' by Herbert Tuttle. 2 vols. 1888.   (*S.R.* July.)

Dickens as an Actor.   (*M.G.* March 5.)

The Emperor William and Princess Radziwill. Tr. from Treitschke.
                                                    (*M.G.* March 12.)

Nichol's "Tables of History." Review.   (*M.G.* March 12.)

Review of 'William the Conqueror,' by Edward A. Freeman. (Twelve English Statesmen Series.)   (*M.G.* April 16.)

The late Matthew Arnold. (Leading Article.)   (*M.G.* April 17.)

1889

The Counter-Reformation. (Epochs of Church History.)

Elizabeth, Queen of Bohemia.   (*D.N.B.* vol. XVII.)

George Faulkner, 1790?–1862.   (*D.N.B.* vol. XVIII.)

Elizabeth Cleghorn Gaskell.   (*D.N.B.* vol. XXI.)

George I, King of England.   (*D.N.B.* vol. XXI.)

George, Prince of Denmark.   (*D.N.B.* vol. XXI.)

Address on Open Night of Manchester Goethe Society, Nov. 22.
                                                    (*Academy,* Dec. 7.)

Review of 'Neuchâtel et la Politique prussienne en Franche-Comté (1702–1713). D'après des documents inédits des Archives de Paris, Berlin, et Neuchâtel,' par Emile Bourgeois. (Bibliothèque de la Faculté des Lettres de Lyon, tome I.) 1887.
                                                    (*E.H.R.* April.)

*Review of 'L'Acquisition de la couronne Royale de Prusse par les Hohenzollern,' par Albert Waddington. (Bibliothèque de la Faculté des Lettres de Lyon, tome IX.) 1888.   (*E.H.R.* July.)

Review of 'Scharnhorst,' von Max Lehmann. 2 Bde. 1886–7.
                                                    (*E.H.R.* Oct.)

Review of 'Essays of the late Mark Pattison, sometime Rector of Lincoln College'; collected and arranged by Henry Nettleship. 2 vols. 1889.   (*E.H.R.* Oct.)

A Rabelais manqué? ('Ath. Gasker.')

(*Owens College Mag.* Oct.)

*Godolphin. Review of 'The life of Sidney, Earl of Godolphin, K.G., Lord High Treasurer of England, 1702–1710,' by the Hon. Hugh Elliot. 1888.   (*S.R.* Feb. 2.)

A French Biography of Dickens. Review of 'Un Maître du roman contemporain. L'inimitable Boz. Étude historique et anecdotique sur la vie et l'œuvre de Charles Dickens,' par Robert du Pontavice de Heussey. 1889.   (*M.G.* March 29.)

Review of 'The London Stage: its history and traditions from 1576 to 1888,' by H. Barton Baker. 2 vols.   (*M.G.* April 23.)

Mr Gardiner's New Volume. Review of 'History of the Great Civil War, 1642–9,' by Samuel R. Gardiner, etc. Vol. II. 1644–7.   (*M.G.* April 24.)

Review of 'The true story of the Catholic Hierarchy deposed by Queen Elizabeth; with fuller memoirs of the last two survivors,' by T. E. Bridgett and T. F. Knox.   (*M.G.* Oct. 8.)

Review of 'Behind the scenes of the Comédie Française and other recollections,' by Arsène Houssaye; trans. and ed. with notes by Albert D. Vandam.   (*M.G.* Oct. 22.)

Courthope's "Life of Pope." Review of 'The life of Alexander Pope,' by William John Courthope. (The Works of Alexander Pope. New edition, including new materials collected in part by the Rt. Hon. J. Wilson Croker; with introduction and notes by Whitwell Elwin and W. J. Courthope. Vol. v. Life and index.)   (*M.G.* Nov. 13.)

[Paper on Count William of Schaumburg-Lippe. Manchester Goethe Society, Dec. 11.]

1890

*Review of 'Politische und militärische Correspondenz König Friedrichs von Würtemberg mit Kaiser Napoleon I, 1805–1813'; herausgegeben von A. von Schlossberger. 1889.— 'König Friedrich von Würtemberg und seine Zeit,' von Albert Pfister. 1888.—'Mömpelgard's schöne Tage,' von Otto Schanzenbach. 1887.   (*E.H.R.* Jan.)

The Universities and the Counter-Reformation.
                                    (*Macmillan's Mag.* Nov.)

Review of 'The Christmas Carol,' by Charles Dickens; a facsimile reproduction of the author's original MS., with an introduction by F. G. Kitton.   (*M.G.* Oct. 21.)

Lord Houghton. Review of 'The life, letters and friendships of Richard Monckton Milnes, First Lord Houghton,' by T. Wemyss Reid. 2 vols.   (*M.G.* Dec. 10.)

[Address. Victoria University Theological degrees, May and November.

Address. Opening of Owens College Arts Department, October.

An old-fashioned Debating Problem. Address at Owens College Debating Society, October.

Address. Southern Hospital, Manchester, October.

Address. Oxford and Cambridge Local Examinations, October.

Goethe, Bürger, and Müllner. Paper to Manchester Goethe Society, Dec. 3.]

1891

John Heywood.   (*D.N.B.* vol. xxvi.)

Thomas Heywood, d. 1650?   (*D.N.B.* vol. xxvi.)

Anne Hyde, Duchess of York.   (*D.N.B.* vol. xxviii.)

Henry Hyde, Second Earl of Clarendon.   (*D.N.B.* vol. xxviii.)

Henry, Lord Hyde   (*D.N.B.* vol. xxviii.)

Jane Hyde, Countess of Clarendon and Rochester.
                                                  (*D.N.B.* vol. xxviii.)

Lawrence Hyde, Earl of Rochester.   (*D.N.B.* vol. xxviii.)

James II, King of England.   (*D.N.B.* vol. xxix.)

William Stanley Jevons.   (*D.N.B.* vol. xxix.)

Review of 'Briefe der Kurfürstin Sophie von Hannover an die
    Raugräfinnen und Raugrafen zu Pfalz'; herausgegeben von
    Eduard Bodemann. (Publ. aus den K. Preuss. Staatsarchiven,
    Bd. xxxvii.) 1888.   (*E.H.R.* Jan.)

Review of 'The Swedish revolution under Gustavus Vasa,' by Paul
    Barron Watson. 1889.   (*E.H.R.* April.)

Review of 'Geschichte der deutschen Verfassungsfrage während
    der Befreiungskrieg und des Wiener Kongresses, 1812 bis 1815,'
    von Wilhelm Adolf Schmidt. Aus dessen Nachlass, herausgegeben
    von Alfred Stern. 1890.   (*E.H.R.* July.)

[Manchester Day Training College. Address to meeting of Stock-
    port Association of Members, March.

Fitzgerald, Spedding, and Donne. Address to the St Paul's Literary
    Society, April.

Address at Opening of Bolton High School Buildings by Mrs
    Fawcett, May.

Address at Opening of Fallowfield Bazaar, November.

Address on Day Training Colleges, Blackburn, November.

Address to Owens College Debating Society, 30th Anniversary,
    Dec. 11.]

1892

Samuel Johnson, 1691–1773.   (*D.N.B.* vol. xxx.)

Louise Renée de Kerouaille, Duchess of Portsmouth.
                        (*D.N.B.* vol. xxxi.)

George Lillo.   (*D.N.B.* vol. xxxiii.)

Speech on Proposed College of Music.   (*M.G.* Oct. 8.)

Address to Oldham District Teachers' Association, at Oldham, St Domingo Street Schools, Oct. 28.   (*M.G.* Oct. 29.)

**A Study of Good Women.* (Monday Popular Lecture at Owens College.)   (*M.G.* Nov. 8.)

Review of 'History of the Great Civil War, 1642–1649,' by Samuel R. Gardiner. Vol. iii. 1891.—'A student's history of England from the earliest times to 1885,' by Samuel Rawson Gardiner. 1892.   (*E.H.R.* July.)

Review of 'Correspondance secrète du Comte de Mercy-Argenteau avec l'Empereur Joseph II et le Prince de Kaunitz'; publiée par le Chevalier d'Arneth et J. Flammermont. 2 tomes. 1889–91.   (*E.H.R.* Oct.)

My Peterhouse Days.   (*The Grayling,* no. ii, Oct.)

The History of David Grieve. Review of 'The history of David Grieve,' by Mrs Humphry Ward.   (*M.G.* March.)

The late Mr Freeman.   (Leader, *M.G.* March 18.)

On a Recent Academical Appointment.   (*M.G.* April 9.)

Three Short Letters on Infirmary Question.
                        (*M.G.* July and Aug.)

Two letters to the *Times.* 'The Albert University.' (Jan. 30.)— 'The proposed Gresham University.' (Feb. 26.)

Old English Drama. 3rd ed. Revised. Oxford.

[Address to Christian Evidence Society Annual Meeting, May 1.

Speech at Town Hall. Banquet to Lord Spencer as Chancellor of Victoria University, May 26.

Address at Opening of Ladywell Sanatorium, Salford, June.

Report to Manchester Chamber of Commerce on Commercial Teaching, Dec.

Speeches at Opening of Victoria Buildings, University College, Liverpool, Dec.]

1893

Mary II, Queen of England.   (*D.N.B.* vol. xxxvi.)

Mary of Modena.   (*D.N.B.* vol. xxxvi.)

Address at Annual Meeting of Victoria Dental Hospital, Feb. 13.
                                                (*M.G.* Feb. 14.)

Address at Annual Meeting of Manchester Social Club, Feb. 15.
                                                (*M.G.* Feb. 16.)

Address to St Paul's Literary and Educational Society at their Jubilee, Sept. 29.   (*M.G.* Sept. 30.)

Address at Opening of Royal Manchester College of Music, Oct. 7.
                                                (*M.G.* Oct. 9.)

Address to the Chancellor of the Exchequer at Deputation from University Colleges, Nov. 21.   (*Times* and *M.G.* Nov. 22.)

Address at Bolton Grammar School on Secondary Education, Dec. 19.
                                                (*M.G.* Dec. 20.)

Review of 'Elisabeth Farnese, the Termagant of Spain,' by Edward Armstrong. 1892.   (*E.H.R.* Jan.)

Short notice of 'The Life and Works of John Arbuthnot,' by George A. Aitken. 1892.   (*E.H.R.* Jan.)

Review of 'Ein hannoversch-englischer Offizier vor hundert Jahren. Christian Friedrich Wilhelm Freiherr von Ompteda, Oberst und Brigadier in der Königlich Deutschen Legion. 26. November 1765 bis 18. Juni 1815,' von Ludwig Freiherr von Ompteda. 1892.   (*E.H.R.* April.)

Anton Gindely.   (*E.H.R.* July.)

Short Notices: Review of 'Entstehung und erste Entwicklung der Katechismen des seligen Petrus Canisius.' Geschichtlich dargelegt von Otto Braunsberger. 1893.—'Diary of Samuel Pepys,' ed. by Henry B. Wheatley. Vol. i. 1893.—'Navy Record Society.' (Short account of preliminary meeting.) (*E.H.R.* July.)

Review of 'Corrispondenza tra L. A. Muratori e G. G. Leibniz, conservata nella R. Biblioteca di Hannover ed in altri Instituti, e pubblicata da Matteo Campori.' 1892.   (*E.H.R.* Oct.)

Review of 'La Fin d'une Société. Le Duc de Lauzun et la Cour Intime de Louis XV,' par Gaston Maugras. 1893.
                                    (*E.H.R.* Oct.)

Review of 'The works of John Dryden; illustrated with notes, etc., by Sir Walter Scott,' revised by George Saintsbury. Vols. xvii and xviii. 1892–3.   (*S.R.* Nov. 11.)

Review of 'Carmina Mariana: An English anthology in verse in honour of or in relation to the Blessed Virgin Mary,' corrected and arranged by Orby Shipley.   (*M.G.* June 20.)

Review of 'The works of John Dryden, illustrated with notes, etc., and a life of the author by Sir Walter Scott.' Revised and corrected by George Saintsbury. Vols. xvii and xviii.
                                    (*M.G.* Nov. 7.)

Letter to the *Times* (The Victoria University), July 17.

Sir Philip Sidney.—Thomas Lodge.—Robert Greene.—Thomas Nash. In Sir H. Craik's "English Prose Selections," vol. i.

4–2

[Address at North Manchester High School for Girls, April 19.

Address at Opening of Mauldeth Hospital for Incurables, May.

Speech at Victoria University Court, B.A. degrees for Theological Students, May 18.

Address at Annual Meeting of S.P.C.K., June.

Speech at Farewell Dinner to Professor Adamson, June 29.

Address at Withington High School for Girls, July 4.

Lauder v. Milton; with some thoughts on Plagiarism. Paper read to Owens College Shakespeare Society, Nov. 24.

Address at Meeting of Strangeways Refuge at Rusholme Town Hall.]

1894

Goethe, Bürger, and Müllner; and Abstracts of other papers read before the Manchester Goethe Society. (Transactions of the Manchester Goethe Society, 1886–1893.) Manchester.

Address at the Opening of the Gorton Branch Free Public Library, May 5. (*M.G.* May 7.)

Address at Opening of Owens College Session, Oct. 2. (*M.G.* Oct. 3.)

Address at Opening of Yorkshire College Session, Oct. 16. (*Leeds Mercury*, Oct. 17.)

The Poems of Bishop Ken. Lecture to the Owens College Literary Society, Nov. 2.   (Pr. in *Coll. Papers*, vol. IV, 1921.)

Review of 'Calendar of Letters and State Papers relating to English affairs, preserved principally in the Archives of Simancas'; ed. by Martin A. S. Hume. Vol. I. Elizabeth, 1558–1567. 1892.
(*E.H.R.* Jan.)

Review of 'Markgraf Ludwig Wilhelm von Baden und der Reichs-
krieg gegen Frankreich, 1693–1697; herausgegeben von der
Badischen Kommission.' Bearbeitet von Aloys Schulte. 2 Bde.
1892.   (*E.H.R.* Jan.)

Review of 'The City-State of the Greeks and Romans: a survey
introductory to the study of ancient history,' by W. Warde
Fowler. 1893.   (*E.H.R.* April.)

Review of 'Venetianische Depeschen vom Kaiserhofe (Dispacci di
Germania). Herausgegeben von der Historischen Commission
der königlichen Akademie der Wissenschaften.' Bearbeitet von
Gustav Turba. Bd. II. 1892.   (*E.H.R.* April.)

Review of 'Briefe und Tagebücher Georg Forster's von seiner
Reise am Niederrhein, in England und in Frankreich im Früh-
jahr 1790.' Herausgegeben von Albert Leitzmann. 1893.
(*E.H.R.* July.)

Review of 'Die Augsburger Allianz von 1686,' von Richard Fester.
1893.   (*E.H.R.* Oct.)

Review of 'Maria Landgräfin von Hessen, geborene Prinzessin
von England,' von Erich Meyer. 1894.   (*E.H.R.* Oct.)

The Bishop of Peterborough's "History of the Papacy," vol. v. Review
of 'A history of the Papacy during the period of the Reformation,' by M Creighton. Vol. v.—The German revolt, 1517–
1527. 1894.   (*S.R.* March 17.)

Marcella. Review of 'Marcella,' by Mrs Humphry Ward. 1894.
(*M.G.* April 2.)

Review of 'Caligula: eine Studie über römischen Caesarenwahn-
sinn,' von L. Quidde. 16te Auflage.   (*M.G.* July 10.)

The Spider and the Flie. By John Heywood. With introduction
by A. W. W. (Spenser Society.) Manchester.

*Ben Jonson.—Sir Henry Wotton.—John Earle.—John Milton.—
Abraham Cowley.* In Sir H. Craik's "English Prose Selections,"
vol. II.

*Halifax.—*Lady Mary Wortley Montagu.* In Sir H. Craik's
"English Prose Selections," vol. III.

[Speech as Chairman of Dr Tatham's Farewell Dinner, Jan. 18.

Elizabeth of Bohemia. Lecture at University College, Liverpool,
March 16.

Answers to Secondary Education Commission. (With Dr Wilkins.)
May.

Address to the Queen, on her Visit to Manchester. Presented at
the School of Art, May 21.

Address on Opening of Ardwick Higher Grade Board School,
Oct. 19.

Heads of Evidence before Royal Commission on Secondary Education. (Evidence given Oct. 23.)

Address to the Duke of Devonshire on his Visit to Owens College
on Opening of New Medical Buildings, Nov. 6.

Address at the Distribution of Prizes to the Manchester Clerks'
and Warehousemen's Schools, Cheadle Hulme, Nov. 17.

Speech at Mr Armitage's Dinner to Mr Bayard, Dec. 16.]

1894–1912

The Poems of John Byrom. Edited, with introduction, by A. W. W.
(Chetham Society.) 3 vols. Manchester.

1895

John Oldham, 1653–1683.   (*D.N.B.* vol. XLII.)
George Peele.   (*D.N.B.* vol. XLIV.)

Review of 'Zur Verhaftung des Landgrafen Philipp von Hessen,' von Gustav Turba. 1894.   (*E.H.R.* Jan.)

Review of 'Periods of European history. V. Europe, 1598–1715,' by Henry Offley Wakeman. 1894.   (*E.H.R.* Jan.)

Review of 'The diary of Samuel Pepys; with Lord Braybrooke's notes'; ed., with additions, by Henry B. Wheatley. Vols. III and IV. 1893–4.   (*E.H.R.* Jan.)

Review of 'Un Paladin au XVIIIme siècle: le Prince Charles de Siegen, d'après sa correspondance originale et inédite de 1784 à 1789,' par le Marquis D'Aragon. 1893.   (*E.H.R.* Jan.)

Review of 'König Ludwig II von Bayern: ein Beitrag zu seiner Lebensgeschichte,' von C. von Heigel. 1893.   (*E.H.R.* Jan.)

Review of 'Der Ursprung des Planes vom ewigen Frieden in den Memoiren des Herzogs von Sully,' von Theodor Kükelhaus. 1893.   (*E.H.R.* April.)

Review of 'Der niedersächsisch-dänische Krieg,' von Julius Otto Opel. III. 1894.   (*E.H.R.* April.)

Review of 'The Marquis d'Argenson: a study in criticism,' by Arthur Ogle. (Stanhope Essay, 1893.) 1893.   (*E.H.R.* April.)

*Review of 'The memoirs of Edmund Ludlow, Lieutenant-General of the Horse in the Army of the Commonwealth of England, 1625–1672'; ed., with appendices of letters and illustrative documents, by C. H. Firth. 2 vols. 1894.   (*E.H.R.* July.)

Review of 'Die Würzburger Hilfstruppen im Dienste Oesterreichs, 1756–1763,' von L. Freiherrn von Thüna. 1893.   (*E.H.R.* July.)

Review of 'Geschichte des letzten Ministeriums Königin Annas von England (1710–1714) und der englischen Thronfolgefrage,' von Felix Salomon. 1894.   (*E.H.R.* Oct.)

The late Dr Hager. (With Dr Wilkins.)   (*M.G.* Feb. 23.)

*_The Life and Letters of E. A. Freeman._ Review of 'The life and letters of Edward A. Freeman,' by W. R. W. Stephens. 2 vols.
(_M.G._ May 20.)

Review of 'The story of Bessie Costrell,' by Mrs Humphry Ward.
(_M.G._ July 2.)

Short Leader on the Empress Eugénie and Heinrich von Sybel.
(_M.G._ July 8.)

Edward FitzGerald. Review of 'Letters of Edward FitzGerald to Fanny Kemble, 1871–1883'; edited by William Aldis Wright.
(_M.G._ Nov. 2.)

[Address. White Cross League, June 27.

Vice-Chancellor's Annual Statement, June 29.

Address (Technical Education) at Stockport Technical School, Nov. 13.

Address to Lord Mayor of Manchester on Presentation of Mace, Dec. 17.

Memorial to Sir M. Hicks Beach on University College Grant. (With Dr Bodington.) Presented Dec. 20.]

1896

William Pulteney, Earl of Bath.	(_D.N.B._ vol. XLVII.)
Hannah Mary Rathbone.	(_D.N.B._ vol. XLVII.)
Edward Ravenscroft.	(_D.N.B._ vol. XLVII.)

Contribution to Knight's " Life of J. P. Nichol."

Review of 'Le Roman d'une Impératrice: Catherine II de Russie, d'après ses mémoires, sa correspondance et les documents inédits des Archives d'État,' par K. Waliszewski. 1893.—'Autour d'une Trône. Catherine II de Russie: ses collaborateurs, ses amis, ses favoris,' par K. Waliszewski. 1894.   (_E.H.R._ Jan.)

Review of 'The journal of Joachim Hane, containing his escapes and sufferings during his employment by Oliver Cromwell in France from November 1653 to February 1654'; ed. from the manuscript in the library of Worcester College, Oxford, by C. H. Firth. 1896.   (*E.H.R.* July.)

Review of 'Le Père Joseph et Richelieu,' par Gustave Fagniez. 2 tomes. 1894.—'Le Père Joseph Polémiste: ses premiers écrits,' par L. Dedouvres. 1895.   (*E.H.R.* Oct.)

Mrs Humphry Ward's new novel. Review of 'Sir George Tressady,' by Mrs Humphry Ward.   (*M.G.* Sept. 25.)

The St Mary's and Southern Hospitals and the Lewis Trustees.
                    (*M.G.* Nov. 17.)

The Manchester Royal Infirmary. Letter on Manchester Infirmary Question (Owens College). (With Mr Thompson.)
                    (*M.G.* Dec. 12.)

Charles Dickens.—Mrs Gaskell. In Sir H. Craik's "English Prose Selections," vol. v.

[Speech at Dinner of Institution of British Architects.

Speech at Dublin University Dinner (Mr E. H. Lecky).

Address on Opening of Winter Session of Manchester School of Domestic Economy and Cookery (with Bishop of Manchester), Jan. 16.

Speech at Preston High School for Girls, Feb. 17.

Vice-Chancellor's Annual Statement, June 27.

Revision of Rules of Cancer Pavilion and Home, July.

Revision of Rules of University Settlement, July.

Address at Ardwick Green Industrial School Prize Distribution, July 21.

Vice-Chancellor's Speech to Court on Resignation, Nov. 12.

Address at Bury Grammar School Prize Distribution, Nov. 18.

Address at Oldham Girls School Prize Distribution, Nov. 20.

Address at Withington Girls School, Nov. 28.

Address at Stockport Grammar School Distribution of Prizes, Dec. 18.]

1897

Lord William and Lady Rachel Russell.   (*D.N.B.* vol. XLIX.)

Ehrengard Melusina von der Schulenburg, Duchess of Kendal.

                                  (*D.N.B.* vol. L.)

James Scott, Duke of Monmouth.   (*D.N.B.* vol. LI.)

Sir Charles Sedley.   (*D.N.B.* vol. LI.)

Henry Shirley.   (*D.N.B.* vol. LII.)

James Shirley.   (*D.N.B.* vol. LII.)

Thomas Southerne.   (*D.N.B.* vol. LIII.)

Address to Headmasters Association on University Colleges and Secondary Schools (Burnley), March 6.   (*M.G.* March 8.)

Queen's Commemoration. Executive Committee's Appeal to Citizens of Manchester, March 27.

Speech on conferring of Freedom of City of Manchester, Oct. 27.

                                  (*M.G.* Oct. 28.)

Review of 'Die Regierung der Königin Maria Stuart von England, 1689–1695,' von W. K. A. Nippold. 1895.   (*E.H.R.* Jan.)

Review of 'The balance of power, 1715–1789,' by Arthur Hassall. (Periods of European History.) 1896.   (*E.H.R.* April.)

Review of 'La Mission de M. de Gontaut-Biron à Berlin,' par le Duc de Broglie. 1896.   (*E.H.R.* April.)

Review of 'Venetianische Depeschen vom Kaiserhofe (Dispacci di Germania); herausgegeben von der Historischen Commission der kaiserlichen Akademie der Wissenschaften.' Bearbeitet von Gustav Turba. Bd. III. 1895.   (*E.H.R.* July.)

*Review of 'Englische Geschichte im achtzehnten Jahrhundert,' von Wolfgang Michael. Bd. 1. 1896.   (*E.H.R.* July.)

Review of 'Les Portefeuilles du Président Bouhier: extraits de fragments de correspondances littéraires,' par Emmanuel de Broglie. 1896.   (*E.H.R.* July.)

Review of 'Verhaftung und Gefangenschaft des Landgrafen Philipp von Hessen (1547–1550),' von Gustav Turba. 1896.
                    (*E.H.R.* Oct.)

The Early Years of Heinrich von Treitschke. Review of 'Heinrich von Treitschkes Lehr- und Wanderjahre 1834–1866,' von Theodor Schiemann. 1896.   (*M.G.* Jan.)

Sir M. E. Grant Duff's "Reminiscences." Review of 'Notes from a Diary, 1851–1872,' by the Rt Hon. Sir Mountstuart E. Grant Duff. 2 vols.   (*M.G.* Feb. 12.)

Review of 'Poems of Thomas Hood'; ed. by Alfred Ainger. 2 vols.   (*M.G.* Nov. 16.)

Heinrich von Sybel. Review of 'Vorträge und Abhandlungen.' Mit einer biographischen Einleitung von C. Varrentrapp. 1897.
                    (*M.G.* Dec.)

**A Woman Killed with Kindness.* T. Heywood. Edited, with introduction, by A. W. W. (Temple Dramatists Series.)

Revision etc. of Clavigo. Translated by members of the Manchester Goethe Society.

[Speech at Luncheon to the Duke of Devonshire in Manchester Town Hall on Opening of Tudor Exhibition, April 29.

Speech in Chair at Annual Meeting of Chetham Society, May 28.

Address at Reception of School Board Clerks Conference at Owens College, June 9.

Speech at Meeting of Victoria University Court. Motion as to Privileged Institutions, June 14.

Speech on Presenting Rt Hon. James Bryce for Victoria University Degree of Litt.D., July 3.

Address to American Librarians on their Visit to Owens College, July 8.

Observations at Secondary Education Conference (Victoria University), July 10.

Owens College Opening Meeting and Court Speeches, Oct. 5.

Address to Sunday School Teachers in Holy Innocents Church, Fallowfield, Dec. 12.

Lecture on Sir Henry Wotton at Owens College, Dec. 13.

Address at Prize Distribution of Municipal Technical School and School of Art in Manchester Town Hall, Dec. 21.]

1898

Sir Henry Wotton. A Biographical Sketch.

Charles Talbot, Duke of Shrewsbury.   (*D.N.B.* vol. LV.)

John Edward Taylor.   (*D.N.B.* vol. LV.)

The late Thomas Ashton. 1898.
          (*Manchester Lit. and Phil. Soc. Mem. and Proc.* 1897–8.)

Review of 'La torture aux Pays-Bas autrichiens pendant le XVIIIe siècle: son application, ses partisans, et ses adversaires,' par Eugène Hubert. 1897.   (*E.H.R.* Jan.)

Review of 'Maupertuis et ses correspondants: lettres inédites du Grand Frédéric, du Prince Henri de Prusse, de La Beaumelle, etc.,' par A. Le Sueur. 1897.   (*E.H.R.* Jan.)

Short notice of 'Danmark's Riges Historie.'   (*E.H.R.* Jan.)

*Review of 'Der Grosse Kurfürst Friedrich Wilhelm von Brandenburg,' von Martin Philippson. Teil 1. 1640 bis 1660. 1897.
          (*E.H.R.* April.)

Review of 'Joseph II et la liberté de l'Escaut.—La France et l'Europe,' par F. Magnette. 1897.   (*E.H.R.* April.)

Review of 'Le Comte de Vergennes: son Ambassade en Suède, 1771–1774,' par Louis Bonneville de Marsangy. 1898.
(*E.H.R.* July.)

Review of 'Erlebnisse in Marburg, 1688–1695,' von Denis Papin. 1898.   (*E.H.R.* July.)

*Review of 'Louis XV et le renversement des alliances; préliminaires de la guerre de sept ans, 1754–1756,' par Richard Waddington. 1896.   (*E.H.R.* Oct.)

By Way of Prologue. (*The Goal Post*, No. 1. Owens College Students' Bazaar, December.)

Mr Thomas Ashton.   (*M.G.* Jan. 22.)

Review of 'History of England for the use of Middle Forms of schools,' by Professors York Powell and Tout. Pt II, by Professor Tout.   (*M.G.* Feb. 8.)

Prince William of Prussia and the Princess Radziwil.
(*M.G.* Feb. 15.)

*George Brandes' " Life of Shakspere." Review of 'William Shakspere; a critical biography,' by George Brandes. 2 vols.
(*M.G.* March 3.)

English Religious Pamphlets. Review of 'Religious pamphlets'; selected and arranged by Percy Dearmer, with introduction and notes. (Pamphlet Library.)   (*M.G.* March 17.)

Mrs Humphry Ward's New Story. Review of 'Helbeck of Bannisdale,' by Mrs Humphry Ward.   (*M.G.* June 10.)

The University Settlement in Ancoats.   (*M.G.* June 25.)

*Helen Faucit (Lady Martin). Obituary Notice.   (*M.G.* Nov. 1.)

Bismarck under Frederick William IV. Review of 'Gedanken u. Erinnerungen von Fürst Otto von Bismarck.' Bd. 1.
(*M.G.* Dec.)

Professor Mahaffy and the Victoria University.
(*Times*, March 23 and 28.)

[Speeches (valedictory) at College and Associates Dinners, and at presentation of Mr Herkomer's portrait, March 1; also at Southern Hospital Annual Meeting, Feb. 25.

Valedictory Speech to Owens College Union on Presentation of "Biographie Générale" and bookcase, March 24; and to Women's Department on presentation to Mrs Ward, May 9.

Speech at Opening of Christie Library at Owens College, June 22.]

1899

A History of English Dramatic Literature to the Death of Queen Anne. New and revised edition. 3 vols.

Great Britain and Hanover. Some aspects of the Personal Union. (Ford Lectures, 1899.) German translation by K. Woltereck, Hanover, 1906.

Horatio Walpole, Baron Walpole of Wolterton.
(*D.N.B.* vol. LIX.)

William Walsh, 1663–1708.   (*D.N.B.* vol. LIX.)

John Ward, 1805–1890.   (*D.N.B.* vol. LIX.)

Paul Whitehead.   (*D.N.B.* vol. LXI.)

William Whitehead.   (*D.N.B.* vol. LXI.)

William III, King of England.   (*D.N.B.* vol. LXI.)

Some Suggestions of the Renascence. Address at the Opening Session of Bedford College for Women, York Place, London, Oct. 10.
(*Bedford College Mag.* Dec.)

Remarks on Molière's "Don Juan."
(*Elizabethan Stage Society Programme,* Dec. 15.)

Review of 'Zur Vorgeschichte des Orleans'schen Krieges. Nuntia-
turberichte aus Wien und Paris, 1685–1688. Herausgegeben
von der Badischen Historischen Kommission.' Bearbeitet von
Max Immach, mit einem Vorworte von F. von Weech. 1898.
(*E.H.R.* Jan.)

Review of 'L'État et les églises en Prusse sous Frédéric-Guillaume
Ier, 1713–1740,' par Georges Pariset. 1897.   (*E.H.R.* Jan.)

Note on 'Un Anonyme du XVIIe siècle,' par A. Waddington.
1898.   (*E.H.R.* Jan.)

Note on 'Kensington Palace,' by W. J. Loftie. 1898. (*E.H.R.* Jan.)

Review of 'Europe in the sixteenth century, 1494–1598,' by
A. H. Johnson. (Periods of European History.) 1897.
(*E.H.R.* April.)

Review of 'Letters of Princess Elizabeth of England, daughter of
King George III and Landgravine of Hesse-Homberg, written
for the most part to Miss Louisa Swinburne'; ed. by Philip C.
Yorke. 1898.   (*E.H.R.* April.)

Short notice of two programmes of the Königsstadt Realgymnasium
in Berlin by F. Hirsch, 'Brandenburg and England, 1674–1679.'
(*E.H.R.* July.)

Short notice of R. S. Rait's 'Report to the new Spalding Club
on the Burnett MSS. in the Archives of State at Hanover and the
Marshal Keith letters in the Royal Library at Berlin.' 1898.
(*E.H.R.* July.)

Review of 'Deutsche Geschichte im Zeitalter der Gegenreforma-
tion,' von Gustav Wolf. Bd. I. 1898, 1899.   (*E.H.R.* Oct.)

Review of 'The Diary of Samuel Pepys'; ed. by Henry S. Wheatley.
Vols. v–viii; with supplementary volume, 'Pepysiana and index
volume.' 1895–1899.   (*E.H.R.* Oct.)

Sir M. E. Grant Duff's "Indian Reminiscences." Review of 'Notes
from a Diary,' by Rt Hon. Sir M. E. G. Duff.
(*M.G.* March 18.)

Christie's "Étienne Dolet." A New Edition. Review of 'Étienne Dolet, the martyr of the Renaissance, 1508–1546, a biography,' by Richard Copley Christie. New ed., revised and corrected.
(M.G. Oct. 3.)

Mr Gosse's "Donne." Review of 'The life and letters of John Donne, Dean of St Paul's'; now for the first time revised and corrected by Edmund Gosse. 2 vols.   (<i>M.G.</i> Oct. 28.)

[Speech on Admission of Women to the Medical School. Owens College Court of Governors, Oct. 3.]

1900

Presidential Address to Royal Historical Society, Feb. 1.
(Royal Hist. Soc. Trans., N.S. XIV.)

Mary Anne Everett Wood, afterwards Mrs Everett Green.
(D.N.B. vol. LXII.)

Wallenstein and the Piccolomini.
(Elizabethan Stage Society Programme, July.)

Review of 'Spain, its Greatness and Decay (1479–1788),' by Martin A. S. Hume; with an introduction by Edward Armstrong. (Cambridge Historical Series.) 1898.   (*E.H.R.* Jan.)

Review of 'Correspondance inédite du Général-Major de Martange, Aide de Camp du Prince Xavier de Saxe, Lieutenant-Général des Armées (1756–1782)'; recueillie et publiée, avec introduction et notes, par Charles Bréard. 1898.   (*E.H.R.* Jan.)

Review of 'The daughter of Peter the Great: a history of Russian diplomacy and of the Russian Court under the Empress Elizabeth Petrovna, 1741–1762,' by R. Nisbet Bain. 1899.
(*E.H.R.* April.)

Review of 'Hans Carl von Winterfeldt, ein General Friedrichs des Grossen,' von L. Mollwo. 1899.   (*E.H.R.* July.)

Review of 'Papst Innocenz XI, 1676–1689: Beiträge zur Geschichte seiner Politik und zur Charakteristik seiner Persönlich-
keit,' von Max Immich. 1900.   (*E.H.R.* Oct.)

*The Girlhood of Queen Louisa.   (*Cornhill Mag.* Oct.)

Georg von Bunsen. Review of 'Georg von Bunsen; ein Charakterbild aus den Lager der Besiegten gezeichnet von seiner Tochter,
Marie von Bunsen.' 1900.   (*The Pilot,* Aug. 11).

The Proposed University of Birmingham. (Signed 'Lente.')
(*M.G.* Feb. 24.)

Sir M. E. Grant Duff's "Reminiscences." Review of 'Notes from
a Diary, 1886–8,' by the Rt Hon. Sir Mountstuart E. Grant
Duff. 2 vols.   (*M.G.* March 23.)

The Manchester Stage. Review of 'The Manchester Stage, 1880–
1900: criticisms reprinted from the *Manchester Guardian.*'
(*M.G.* June 1.)

Dr Hannibal Fischer and the German Fleet.   (*M.G.* Aug. 15.)

Review of Mrs Humphry Ward's 'Eleanor.'   (*M.G.* Nov. 2.)

Edmond Rostand's " L'Aiglon."   (*M.G.* Dec. 11.)

Helen Faucit. Review of 'Helena Faucit (Lady Martin),' by
Sir Theodore Martin.   (*M.G.* Dec. 28.)

[Speech at Dinner at Peterhouse on Admission to Mastership,
Oct. 29.

Speech on Proposal to institute Theological Degrees in Victoria
University, Nov. 8.

Speech at Meeting of General Committee for establishing School
of Advanced Historical Studies in London, St Martin's Hall,
Dec. 14.

Report on a Fellowship Essay (King's College), Dec.]

1901

"Tewrdanck" and "Weisskunig," and their Historical Interest. Contributed to "An English Miscellany," presented to Dr Furnivall in honour of his 75th birthday. Oxford.

Richard Copley Christie. (*D.N.B.* Supplement, vol. II.)

Joseph Gouge Greenwood. (*D.N.B.* Supplement, vol. II.)

Remarks on "Everyman" and "Sacrifice of Isaac" (for performance at the Charterhouse), July 13.

Speech at Bury St Edmunds Speech Day, Dec. 16. (Morning Post.)

Sophia Dorothea. Review of 'The love of an uncrowned Queen. Sophia Dorothea, Consort of George I, and her correspondence with Philip Christopher Count Königsmarck. (Now first published from the originals.)' By W. H. Wilkins. 2 vols. 1900.

Review of 'Abhandlungen, Vorträge und Reden,' von Felix Stieve. 1900. (*E.H.R.* Jan.)

Review of 'Essai sur le règne du Prince-Evêque de Liège Maximilien-Henri de Bavière,' par M. Huisman. 1899.
(*E.H.R.* Jan.)

Review of 'Le Drame des Poisons: études sur la Société du XVIIe siècle, et plus particulièrement la Cour de Louis XIV, d'après les Archives de la Bastille,' par F. Funck-Brentano. 1899.
(*E.H.R.* Jan.)

Review of 'La Guerre de Sept Ans; histoire diplomatique et militaire: les débuts,' par Richard Waddington. 1899.
(*E.H.R.* April.)

Short notice of 'Bayern und Hessen, 1799–1816,' von Arthur Kleinschmidt. 1900. (*E.H.R.* April.)

Review of 'Le voyage de l'Empereur Joseph II dans les Pays-Bas (31 Mai 1781—27 Juillet 1781),' par Eugène Hubert. 1890.
(*E.H.R.* July.)

Short notice of 'Mittheilungen der K. Preussischen Archiv-verwaltung'; compiled by Max Bär. 2nd number. 1900.

(*E.H.R.* July.)

Short notice of 'Briefwechsel König Friedrich Wilhelm's III und der Königin Luise mit Kaiser Alexander I'; ed. by P. Bailleu. 1900.   (*E.H.R.* July.)

Review of 'Un Diplomate Français à la Cour Catherine II, 1775–1780: journal intime du Chevalier de Corberon'; publié, avec une introduction et notes, par L. H. Labande. 2 tomes. 1901.

(*E.H.R.* Oct.)

*The Female Rebellion.

(*Owens College Union Mag.* Jubilee Number.)

The Monument to Shakespeare at Weimar. (*Athenaeum,* Dec. 21.)

Renaissance Types. Review of 'Renaissance types,' by William Samuel Lilly.   (*The Pilot,* July 20.)

Mr Richard Copley Christie. (Obituary Notice.) (*M.G.* Jan. 10.)

Dr Gardiner's new volume. Review of 'History of the Common-wealth and Protectorate, 1649–1660,' by Samuel Rawson Gardiner. Vol. III. 1654–1656.   (*M.G.* March 13.)

More Notes from Sir Mountstuart Grant Duff's "Diary." Review of 'Notes from a diary, 1889–1901,' by the Rt Hon. Sir Mount-stuart E. Grant Duff. 2 vols.   (*M.G.* June 10.)

*"Everyman" at the Charterhouse.   (*M.G.* July 17.)

Old English Drama. Fourth edition revised. Oxford.

[Royal Holloway College Special Instruction Committee Repor' (Drafted by A. W. W. from sketch by Lord Thring.) Jan.

Royal Historical Society. Address of Condolence and Congratulation to the King. February.

Observations on Mr Lowes Dickinson's scheme of Political and Economical Studies, Cambridge History Board, April 30.

Speech at Clothworkers Company Dinner, May 1.

Opinions on MSS. for C.U. Press and for Constable and Co. June.

Address to the Hampstead Archaeological Society and others visiting Peterhouse, July 6.

Addresses to Seamen's Mission and Universities Mission to Central Africa, Oct.

University Addresses to the King, the German Emperor and the President of the United States, Nov.

Speech at Dinner to Headmasters Conference, Trinity College, Dec. 20.]

1902

*_Some Aims and Aspirations of European Politics in the_ 19th _century._ Inaugural lecture, Aug. 1, History Section, University Extension Summer Meeting. ("Lectures on the History of the 19th Century.") Cambridge.

*_Elizabeth, Princess Palatine._ (Owens College Historical Essays.) Manchester.

Programme for a Performance of "The Alchemist" by the Elizabethan Stage Society, Aug. 4. Cambridge.

Short notice of Chambonas's 'Souvenirs du Congrès de Vienne,' par Comte A. de la Garde. 1901.   (_E.H.R._ Jan.)

Review of 'Aus dem Briefwechsel König Friedrichs I. von Preussen und seiner Familie'; herausgegeben von Ernst Berner. 1901.
(_E.H.R._ April.)

Review of 'La Mère des Trois Derniers Bourbons, Marie-Josèphe de Saxe, et la Cour de Louis XV,' par Casimir Stryienski. 1902.
(_E.H.R._ July.)

Review of 'Eine Schwester des grossen Kurfürsten, Luise Charlotte, Markgräfin von Brandenburg, Herzogin von Kurland (1617–1676),' von A. Seraphim. 1901.   (*E.H.R.* Oct.)

Review of 'Preussen's auswärtige Politik, 1850–8.' 1902. (Documents left behind by the former Minister-President von Manteuffel and ed. by H. von Poschinger.)   (*E.H.R.* Oct.)

The British Academy. (Occasional notes.)   (*The Pilot*, Jan. 18.)

Professor Adamson. (Letter.)   (*M.G.* Feb. 10.)

**The late Lord Acton.*   (*M.G.* June 23.)

Letter to Mr E. J. Broadfield on Victoria University Question.
          (*M.G.* June 23.)

Mrs Woods' New Play, "The Princess of Hanover."
          (*M.G.* Oct. 7.)

Cambridge and the Licensing Bill.   (*Times*, July 31.)

[Report on a Fellowship Essay. (King's College, Jan. 1.)

Letter to the Duke of Devonshire (Cambridge University Association), May.

Addresses to Seamen's Mission; Choristers Sunday School Prize Distribution, May.

Speech at University Dinner to City Companies, etc., Peterhouse Hall, May 24.

Speech at Luncheon to recipients of Honorary Degrees in Peterhouse Hall, June 10.

University Address to H.M. the King on his Recovery, July.

Vice-Chancellor's Valedictory Speech in Senate House, Oct. 1.

Affidavit for University application of Liverpool to Privy Council, on behalf of Owens College, Manchester, December.]

1902–12

The Cambridge Modern History. Planned by Lord Acton. Edited by A. W. W., G. W. Prothero, Stanley Leathes. 14 vols. Cambridge.

The following are by A. W. W.: Vol. I, chap. XIII. The Netherlands. Vol. III, chap. V. The Empire under Ferdinand I and Maximilian II. Vol. III, chap. XXI. The Empire under Rudolf II. Vol. IV, chap. I. Outbreak of the Thirty Years' War. Vol. IV, chap. III. The Protestant Collapse. Vol. IV, chap. VI. Gustavus Adolphus. Vol. IV, chap. VII. Wallenstein and Bernard of Weimar. Vol. IV, chap. XIII. The Later Years of the Thirty Years' War. Vol. IV, chap. XIV. The Peace of Westphalia. Vol. V, chap. XIV, pt 2. The Peace of Utrecht, etc. Vol. V, chap. XX. The Origins of the Kingdom of Prussia. Vol. V, chap. XXI. The Great Elector and the first Prussian King. Vol. VI, chap. I, pt I. The Hanoverian Succession. Vol. IX, chaps. XIX, XXI. The Congress of Vienna. Vol. XI, chaps. VI, VII. Revolution and Reaction in Germany and Austria. Vol. XIII. Tables and Index. (With Miss A. Greenwood and Miss A. M. Cooke.)

1903

The Electress Sophia and the Hanoverian Succession. (Goupil Illustrated Monograph.) 2nd ed., revised and enlarged, without illustrations, 1909.

*Revision of two Lectures (1891) *on The Regeneration of Germany,* published in "The Development of Modern Philosophy: Remains of Prof. R. Adamson"; edited by Prof. Sorley, vol. II.

Marlowe's "Edward II." Programme for performance at Oxford Summer University Extension Meeting, August 10. (With William Poel.) Oxford.

Speech at Opening of Victoria University of Manchester, Oct. 6.
(*M.G.* Oct. 7.)

Address at Annual Meeting of Chetham Society, Manchester, Oct. 6.
Manchester.   (*Chetham Soc. Trans.*)

*Address at Opening of New Buildings of Withington Girls School,
Manchester, Oct. 7.*   (*M.G.* Oct. 8.)

**An Elizabethan Traveller: Fynes-Moryson.* Review of 'Shake-
speare's Europe: unpublished chapters of Fynes-Moryson's
Itinerary, being a survey of the condition of Europe at the end
of the sixteenth century'; with an introduction and an account
of Fynes-Moryson's career by Charles Hughes. 1903.
                                   (*Edinburgh Rev.* April.)

*Review of 'Der grosse Kurfürst Friedrich Wilhelm von Branden-
burg,' von Martin Philippson. Bd. II. 1902.   (*E.H.R.* Jan.)

Review of 'Die Bayreuther Schwester Friedrichs des Grossen; ein
biographischer Versuch,' von Richard Fester.   (*E.H.R.* Jan.)

Short notice of 'Gustave Adolf's schwedischer Nationalstaat,' von
O. Varenius. German translation published by F. Arnheim.
                                               (*E.H.R.* July.)

Short notice of 'Die Friedensbestrebungen Wilhelms III. von
England in d. J. 1694–1697: ein Beitrag zur Geschichte des
Rijswijker Friedens,' von Gallus Koch. 1903.   (*E.H.R.* July.)

Review of 'Studies in Napoleonic Statesmanship: Germany,' by
Herbert A. L. Fisher. 1903.   (*E.H.R.* Oct.)

Review of 'Louise Grossherzogin von Sachsen-Weimar und ihre
Beziehungen zu den Zeitgenossen,' von E. von Bojanowski.
1903.   (*E.H.R.* Oct.)

Mrs Humphry Ward's new novel, "Lady Rose's Daughter." Review.
                                               (*M.G.* March 5.)

[Speech in Senate House. Economics Tripos Discussion, May 7.

Speech in Guildhall. Annual Meeting of Church Missionary
Society, Cambridge Branch, May 11.

Speech at British Academy. (Thanks to Baron de Bildt.) July.

Speech at Felsted School Prize Distribution, July.

Commemoration of Benefactors, July 7. Peterhouse Chapel; Speech in Hall on the occasion.

Address at Hertford Grammar School Prize Distribution, July 28.

Lecture: "A Study of Good Women," at the opening of King's College Women's Department, Kensington Square, London, Oct. 9.

Speech at Trinity Historical Society Farewell Dinner to S. Leathes, Dec. 9.

Speech at Bury St Edmunds Speech Day, Dec. 22.]

1904

Remarks on Marlowe's "Doctor Faustus." Acted at Guildhall, Cambridge, Nov. 1. Cambridge.

Speech in Whitworth Hall, Manchester University. Presentation of Portraits of Dr Reynolds and Dr Wilkins, Nov. 18.
                                              (*M.G.* Nov. 19.)

*The Letters of Ernst Curtius. Review of 'Ernst Curtius: ein Lebensbild in Briefen,' herausgegeben von Friedrich Curtius. 1903.   (*Edinburgh Rev.* April.)

Review of 'Aus der preussischen Hof- und diplomatischen Gesellschaft,' von A. von Bogulawski. 1903.   (*E.H.R.* Jan.)

Review of 'Le Protestantisme à Tournai pendant le XVIIIᵉ siècle,' par E. Hubert. 1903.   (*E.H.R.* April.)

Review of 'Die Politik der Niederländer während des Kalmerkriegs (1611–1613) und ihr Bündnis mit Schweden (1614) und den Hansestädten (1616),' von Ernst Wiese. 1903. (*E.H.R.* July.)

*Alfred Ainger.   (*Macmillan's Mag.* April.)

John Richard Green. (*Speaker*, Jan. 16.)

Sir Leslie Stephen. (*M.G.* Feb. 23.)

[Speech in Senate House Discussion on Report of Press Syndicate on Partnership Arrangements, Feb. 25.

The late Professor Adamson. Letter to Vice-Chancellor of Victoria University, May.

Speech at the Pepys Society Luncheon, Magdalene College, July 9.

Speech in Peterhouse Hall (Bishop Cosin's portrait), Oct. 29.

Speech in Senate House on Studies Syndicate Report (Abolition of Compulsory Greek), Dec. 1.

Speech in Guildhall on Distribution of Prizes to Perse Girls School, Dec. 8.]

1905

Review of 'Kursächsische Streifzüge,' von O. E. Schmidt.

(*E.H.R.* Jan.)

*Review of 'Der grosse Kurfürst Friedrich Wilhelm von Brandenburg,' von Martin Philippson. Bd. III. 1903. (*E.H.R.* Jan.)

Review of 'La Guerre de Sept Ans: histoire diplomatique et militaire,' par Richard Waddington. Tomes II et III. 1904.

(*E.H.R.* April.)

Review of 'Gedächtnissrede auf Karl Adolf von Cornelius. Gehalten in der K. B. Akademie der Wissenschaften am 12. November 1904,' von Johann Friedrich. 1904. (*E.H.R.* July.)

James VI and the Papacy. Review of 'Clemens VIII. und Jakob I. von England,' von Arnold Oskar Meyer. (Separat-Abdruck aus Quellen und Forschungen aus italien. Archiven und Bibliotheken. Herausgegeben vom K. Preuss. Historischen Institut in Rom.) 1904. (*Scottish Historical Rev.* April.)

Short notice of 'The Life of Margaret Godolphin,' by John Evelyn.
(The King's Classics.) 1903.   (*Church Quarterly Rev.* Oct.)

William Bodham Donne.
                    (*The Speaker*, April 15. Reprinted in *The Burian*.)

The late Professor A. S. Wilkins.   (*M.G.* July 19.)

Compulsory Greek. Letter signed 'Philhellen.'   (*Times*, Feb. 10.)

Higher Education for Business Life.   (*Times*, March 28.)

[Speech in Peterhouse Combination Room: Meeting in support of
University Library Appeal, Jan. 24.

Speech in Senate House on Transference of University Library
books to the Squire Law Library, Feb. 2.

Speeches in Peterhouse Hall at Luncheon to Bishop of Ely and
Lady Alwyne Compton, May 1.

Speech at Leys School (seconding Sir H. Fowler's vote of thanks to
the Duchess of Albany), June 20.

Report on a Fellowship Essay, Trinity College, Sept.

Report on Fellowship Essays, Caius College, Sept.

Speech in Peterhouse Hall at a dinner attended by the new Visitor
(Dr Chase, Bishop of Ely), Oct. 30.

Speech at opening of University Press Buildings in London, Dec. 9.]

1905–7

George Crabbe's Poems. Edited by A. W. W. (With A. T. Bartholomew.) 3 vols. (Cambridge English Classics.) Cambridge.

1906

The late Sir Joshua Fitch. Contribution to A. L. Lilley's "Life of
Sir Joshua Fitch."

Remarks on "The Good Natured Man" (W. Poel's production at
Cambridge University Extension Summer Meeting, July.) Cambridge.

Review of 'L'Auberge des Princes en exil: Anecdotes de la Cour de Bruxelles au XVII^{ieme} siècle,' par Ernest Gossart. 1905.
(*E.H.R.* Jan.)

Short notice of 'The Regency of Marie de Médicis,' by A. P. Lord. 1903.   (*E.H.R.* Jan.)

Short notice of 'Note on the Hanover Princes at Göttingen,' by F. Frensdorff. (Zeitschrift des historischen Vereins für Niedersachsen. 1905, Th. 4.)   (*E.H.R.* April.)

Short notice of 'The Gospel and Human Life: Sermons,' by Alfred Ainger, 1904.   (*Church Quarterly Rev.* Jan.)

Short notice of 'Andrew Marvell,' by Augustine Birrell. (English Men of Letters Series, New Series.) 1905.
(*Church Quarterly Rev.* Jan.)

Short notice of 'Lectures and Essays,' by Alfred Ainger. 2 vols. 1905.   (*Church Quarterly Rev.* July.)

The late Professor Beljame.   (*Athenaeum,* Sept. 29.)

*Dickens as a Social Reformer.
(*National Home Reading Union.   Special Courses Mag.* June.)

The late W. T. Arnold. Review of 'Studies of Roman Imperialism,' by W. T. Arnold; ed. by E. Fiddes; with a memoir of the author by Mrs H. Ward and C. E. Montague.   (*Spectator,* Aug. 25.)

*The Hohenlohe Memoirs. Review of 'Memoirs,' by Prinz Chlodwig zu Hohenlohe-Schillingsfuerst; ed. by F. Curtius. 1906.
(*M.G.* Nov. 5.)

Mrs Gaskell's Works. (Knutsford Edition.) With introductions by A. W. W. 8 vols.

*Lillo's " London Merchant" and " Fatal Curiosity." Edited by A. W. W. (Belles Lettres Series.) Boston, Mass.

[Speech in Senate House (Second Report of Studies Syndicate), April 27.

The Parnassus Plays (Revised paper). Read before Peterhouse Parnassus Club, May.

Speech in Peterhouse Combination Room (Waifs and Strays), May 11.

Speech at Conference in London on Abolition of Teachers' Register, May 12.

Speech at presentation to Professor Gollancz. Christ's College, May 24.

Speech at Trinity Historical Society dinner to Dr Cunningham, Trinity College, May 26.

Speech (French) at Vice-Chancellor's dinner to French University Visitors, Trinity College, June 8.

Speech (German) in Peterhouse Hall. Luncheon to German Newspaper Editors, June 27.

Speech at British Academy, proposing Re-election of Lord Reay as President, June 28.

Speech at University Press Dinner, Holborn Restaurant, London, July 28.

Brief words of Tribute to Mary Bateson. Cambridge Antiquarian Society, Dec. 3.]

1907

Carmen Buriense. School song of King Edward VI's Grammar School. Sung at Bury Pageant (A. N. Parker) July 8 and following days. (With O. L. Richmond.) Bury St Edmunds.

Dr Moritz Brosch.   (*E.H.R.* Oct.)

Short notice of 'Charlotte Brontë and her sisters,' by Clement K. Shorter. (Literary Lives Series.) 1905.

(*Church Quarterly Rev.* Jan.)

A great scholar's life and work. The late Sir Richard Jebb. Review of 'Life and letters of Sir Richard Claverhouse Jebb,' by his wife, Caroline Jebb; with a chapter on Sir Richard Jebb as scholar and critic by A. W. Verrall.   (*M.G.* Oct. 30.)

*Shakespeare's "Henry VI." Parts I, II, III. With introductions by A. W. W. (With Miss A. Greenwood's assistance.) (University Press Shakespeare Renaissance edition.) New York.

[Memorial for F. W. Maitland Pension (with Sir F. Pollock), Jan.

Brief words of Tribute to F. W. Maitland. Royal Historical Society meeting at Lincoln's Inn, Jan. 17.

Short speech at Mrs Frazer's French Plays in Cambridge Theatre, Feb. 13.

Brief words in acknowledgment of Prof. W. Raleigh's Leslie Stephen Lecture, Peterhouse Hall, Feb. 22.

Report on a King's College Fellowship Dissertation, Feb. 23.

Short speeches at Little St Mary's Parish Room (Testimonial to Mr Srawley) and in Peterhouse Combination Room (S.P.C.K. Meeting), March 4 and 6.

Report on an application for Litt.D., May.

Short speech in Peterhouse Hall (Commemoration of Benefactors), May 4.

Short speech in the Senate House (Medieval and Modern Languages Tripos, Amended Report), May 9.

Short speech in St John's Combination Room at Meeting to Establish a Memorial of the late Mary Bateson, May 11.

Short speech in the Senate House (Slade Chair), May 16.

Flysheets: Slade Professorship and Modern Languages Tripos, June.

Few words, Seconding vote of thanks to Lord Reay, British Academy, June 11; Proposing vote of thanks to Sir H. Fowler, Leys School, June 13.

Speech at Jubilee Dinner of Peterhouse Sexcentenary Club, Oct. 28.]

1907–16

The Cambridge History of English Literature. Edited by A. W. W. and A. R. Waller. 14 vols. Cambridge.

The following are by A. W. W.: Vol. v, chap. i. Origins of English Drama. Vol. v, chap. xiv. Some Political and Social Aspects of the later Elizabethan and earlier Stewart Periods. Vol. vi, chap. iv. Thomas Heywood. Vol. vii, chaps. viii, ix. Historical and Political Writings (latter part of the seventeenth century). Vol. viii, chap. i. Dryden. Vol. viii, chap. x (part). Memoir and Letter Writers (late seventeenth century). Vol. viii, chap. xiii (part). Selden's "Table Talk." Vol. ix, chaps. vii, viii. Historical and Political Writers: Burnet and Bolingbroke. Vol. x, chap. xiii. Historians: Gibbon. Vol. xii, chap. xiv. Historians: Writers on Ancient and Early Ecclesiastical History (nineteenth century). Vol. xiii, chap. xi. The Political and Social Novel. Vol. xiv, chap. ii. Historians, Biographers, and Political Orators (nineteenth century).

1908

*Milton Tercentenary. Oration delivered at Burlington House (meeting convened by British Academy), Dec. 8.

Queen Victoria's Letters, 1837–1861. Review of 'The letters of Queen Victoria: a selection of Her Majesty's correspondence between the years 1837 and 1861'; ed. by Arthur Christopher Benson and Viscount Esher. 3 vols. 1907.   (*E.H.R.* Jan.)

Review of 'Kleist-Retzow: ein Lebensbild,' von Hermann von Petersdorff. 1907.   (*E.H.R.* July.)

Review of 'History of England during the Reign of Queen Victoria (1837–1901),' by Sidney Low and Lloyd C. Sanders. (The Political History of England, 12.) 1907. (*E.H.R.* Oct.)

Short notice of 'Die politische und kirchliche Tätigkeit des Monsignor Josef Garampi in Deutschland, 1761–1763,' von J. P. Dengel. 1905.   (*E.H.R.* Oct.)

A New Edition of Evelyn's Diary. Review of 'The diary of John Evelyn'; with an introduction and notes by Austin Dobson. 3 vols. 1906.   (*Church Quarterly Rev.* Jan.)

The Cambridge Modern History. "Cambridge Modern History," translation of a chapter by M. Emile Faguet in vol. v.
                                              (*Athenaeum*, June 20.)

The late Lord Kelvin. (*Cambridge Rev.* Jan. 16. Reprinted in *Peterhouse Sexcentenary Mag.* March.)

The late Master of St John's (Charles Taylor, D.D.).
                                              (*Times*, Aug. 17.)

Marlowe's "Faustus" and Goethe's "Faust," Pt I. (Anster.) With introduction by A. W. W. and notes by C. B. Wheeler. (The World's Classics.) Oxford.

[Flysheets: The Allen Scholarship; The Fitzwilliam Museum; The Oldham Shakespeare Scholarship, Jan. and Feb.

A few words: Bishop of Suffolk Fund Meeting, Peterhouse Combination Room, March 3.

A few words: Prevention of Cruelty to Children, Peterhouse Combination Room, March 11.

A few words: Meeting of Historical Association, Women's Training College, March 14.

A few words: Chancellorship, Private Meeting at Caius, March 30.

Speech (in German) at luncheon to German Theologians given by Divinity Professors at Trinity College, May 29.

A few words: Vote of thanks to Lord Cromer (Leys School), June.

A few words: Vote of thanks to Sir E. Satow (Rede Lecture), June.

A few words: Whitmonday at Cherryhinton, June.

Report to Medieval and Modern Languages Board on an application for a Litt.D. Degree, Nov.

The Heir of Frederick the Great. Paper (revise of Manchester lecture) read to Peterhouse Historical Society, Nov. 4.

Speeches at Manchester University Court and at Chetham Society Annual Meeting, Nov. 13.

Speech (in German) to German Visitors in King's College Hall, Nov. 26.

Short speech at Lord Mayor's Banquet, London, Dec. 9; and at British Academy Meeting (Presidency), Dec. 10.

Speech at Bury School Prize Giving, Dec. 18.]

1909

The Electress Sophia. 2nd ed. (unillustrated), revised and enlarged, with Appendix of Letters of Sophia Dorothea and Königsmarck.

*The Ship of Fools. (Contributed to Fasciculus J. W. Clark dicatus.) Cambridge

Review of 'La Guerre de Sept Ans: histoire diplomatique et militaire,' par Richard Waddington. Tome IV. 1907. (*E.H.R.* Jan.)

Review of 'Onno Klopp: ein Lebenslauf,' von Wiard Klopp. (Jahrbuch der Gesellschaft für bildende Kunst und vaterliche Altertümer zu Emden, XVI.) 1907.   (*E.H.R.* Jan.)

Review of 'Ewald Friedrich, Graf von Hertzberg,' von Andreas Theodor Preuss. 1909.   (*E.H.R.* April.)

Review of 'Luise Ulricke, die schwedische Schwester Friedrichs des Grossen. Ungedrückte Briefe an Mitglieder des preussischen Königshauses.' Herausgegeben von F. Arnheim. Bd. 1. 1909.
(*E.H.R.* July.)

Review of 'A History of Germany, 1715–1815,' by C. T. Atkinson. 1908.   (*E.H.R.* Oct.)

Sir Henry Wotton. Review of 'The life and letters of Sir Henry Wotton,' by Logan Pearsall Smith. 2 vols. 1907. (*Q.R.* Jan.)

F. G. Fleay.   (*Athenaeum,* March 27.)

Preface to S. C. Lomas's edition of Mrs Everett Green's "Life of Elizabeth of Bohemia."

[Inspection of University College, London (Arts), March 16, 17, 18. Report drafted by A. W. W.

Inspection of Bedford College, London (Arts), March 22, 23. Report drafted by A. W. W.

Inspection of King's College, London, May 10–12.

Short speech at Meeting of University Association Committee at Devonshire House for Establishment of a German Professorship at Cambridge, May 17.

Short speech on Presentation of Portrait of Archbishop Maclagan by Bishop of Ely (on behalf of the subscribers) in Peterhouse Combination Room, May 27.

Speech at Prize Giving, Bury School, July 26.

Speech in Senate House Discussion, Medieval and Modern Languages Tripos. English Literature Section, Nov. 18.

Inspection of Royal Holloway College, with Professor Gollancz, Nov. 22, 23.

Inspection of Westfield College, with Prof. Gardner, Nov. 29, 30.

Inspection of East London College, with Prof. Platt, Dec. 6.

Short speech in Peterhouse Combination Room (Schools), Dec. 9.]

1910

Note on 'The Berlin Letters of Sophia Dorothea and Count Königsmarck.'   (*E.H.R.* April.)

Review of 'Anna van Schurman: artist, scholar, saint,' by Una Birch. 1909.   (*E.H.R.* April.)

Review of 'Weltbürgertum und Nationalstaat; Studium zur Genesis des deutschen Nationalstaates,' von F. Meinecke. 1908.
                                                         (*E.H.R.* April.)

Review of 'Dreissig Jahre am Hofe Friedrichs des Grossen. Aus den Tagebüchern des Reichsgrafen Ahasverus Heinrich von Lehndorff, Kammerherrn der Königin Elisabeth Christine von Preussen,' von K. E. Schmidt Lötzen. 1907.   (*E.H.R.* July.)

Review of 'Bismarck und Bayern in der Zeit der Reichsgründung,' von G. Küntzel. (Frankfürter Historische Forschungen, Heft 2.) 1910.   (*E.H.R.* July.)

Review of 'Bayern im Jahre 1866 und die Berufung des Fürsten Hohenlohe'; eine Studie von K. A. von Müller. (Historische Bibliothek, herausgegeben von der Redaktion der Historischen Zeitschrift, Bd. xx.) 1909.   (*E.H.R.* July.)

Review of 'Luise Ulricke, die schwedische Schwester Friedrichs des Grossen. Ungedruckte Briefe an Mitglieder des preussischen Königshauses.' Herausgegeben von Fritz Arnheim. ii. 1747 bis 1758. 1910.   (*E.H.R.* Oct.)

Review of 'Johann Gustav Droysen. Theil i: bis zum Beginn der Frankfürter Tätigkeit,' von G. Droysen. 1910. (*E.H.R.* Oct.)

Short notice of 'Die Deutsche Presse und die Entwicklung der Deutschen Frage 1864–1866,' von Otto Bandmann. (Leipziger Historische Abhandlungen.) 1910.   (*E.H.R.* Oct.)

*Review of 'Geschichte des neueren Dramas,' von Wilhelm Creizenach. Bd. iv, Theil i. 1909.
                                   (*Modern Languages Rev.* July.)

The Oberammergau Play in 1871.   (*Cornhill Mag.* Aug.)

In Memoriam Elizabeth Cleghorn Gaskell.   (*Cornhill Mag.* Oct.)

The late Archbishop Maclagan.

(*Peterhouse Sexcentenary Mag.* Dec.)

Review of 'Mrs Gaskell: haunts, homes and stories,' by Mrs Ellis H. Chadwick.   (*Athenaeum*, Oct. 1.)

[Report on a Dissertation for B.A. Degree, May.

The Oberammergau Passion Play. Paper rewritten for the Parnassus Club, Peterhouse, June 4.

Short speech on First Meeting of Cambridge English Literature Chair Committee (House of Lords), June 15.

Clarendon on Education. Address to the Cambridge Branch of the Assistant Masters Association, June 18.

Speech to Old Peterhouse Men, College Hall, July 12.

Speech as deputy Vice-Chancellor at opening of Pharmaceutical Conference in Botany Theatre, Cambridge, July 26.

Report on a work submitted for Litt.D. Degree, Medieval and Modern Languages Board, Nov.

Short speech in moving Adoption of Court Report, Manchester, Nov. 16.

A few words in the Senate House in Discussion on Establishment of English Literature Professorship, Dec. 8.]

1911

Leibniz as a Politician. Adamson Memorial Lecture in Victoria University of Manchester, Nov. 1910. Manchester.

Presidential Address at British Academy, Oct. 25.

(*British Acad. Proc.*)

*Review of 'Fürst Karl Leiningen und das deutsche Einheitsproblem,' von Veit Valentin. 1910.   (*E.H.R.* Jan.)

Short notice of 'Die Überleitung Preussens in das konstitutionelle System durch den zweiten Vereinigten Landtag,' von Hans Mähl. 1909.   (*E.H.R.* Jan.)

Short notice of 'Die akademische Freiheit in Helmstedt während des 16. und 17. Jahrhunderts,' von Dr Deichert. 1910.
                                        (*E.H.R.* April.)

Short notice of 'Court of Ernest Augustus and Sophia,' by Miss Wendland. (Zeitschrift des Historischen Vereins für Niedersachsen, 1910.)   (*E.H.R.* April.)

Short notice of 'Der Ostpreussische Landtag von 1798,' von Hermann Eicke. 1910.   (*E.H.R.* April.)

Review of 'Friedrich Wilhelm I. und die Volksschule,' von F. Vollmer. 1909.   (*E.H.R.* July.)

*Review of 'Briefe von und an Friedrich von Gentz.' Herausgegeben von Friedrich Carl Wittichen. Bde. I, II. 1909, 1910.
                                        (*E.H.R.* July.)

Review of 'Bunsen und die deutsche Einheitsbewegung,' von W. Ulbricht. (Leipziger Historische Abhandlungen, xx.) 1910.
                                        (*E.H.R.* Oct.)

Review of 'Letters and Journals of Count Charles Leiningen-Westerburg, General in the Hungarian Army'; ed., with an introduction, by Henry Marczali, done into English by Arthur B. Yolland. 1911.   (*E.H.R.* Oct.)

Short notice of 'Piccolomini-Studien,' von O. Elster.
                                        (*E.H.R.* Oct.)

The Dramatic Censorship in Austria. Paragraph on 'Glaube und Heimat von Karl Schönherr.'   (*Athenaeum*, June 10.)

Review of 'Das nachklassische Weimar,' von Adelheid von Schorn.
                                        (*Athenaeum*, Aug. 26.)

**Sir Robert Morier.* Review of 'Memoirs and letters of the Rt Hon. Sir Robert Morier, from 1826 to 1876,' by his daughter, Mrs Rosslyn Wemyss. 2 vols.   (*M.G.* Nov. 23.)

The late F. F. Cornish and Anglo-German Friendship.
(*Times,* May 2.)

Signor Luzzatti and Criticisms on Italy. ("Cambridge Modern
History," vol. XII.) (*Times,* Nov. 18.)

England and Italy (Luzzatti). (*Daily Mail,* Dec. 12.)

[Short speech in Peterhouse Combination Room. Commemoration
of Benefactors, May 13.

Speech in Peterhouse Hall. Dinner to contributors to "Cambridge
Modern History," June 15.

Short speech in Peterhouse Hall. Luncheon to members of the
German and English Goethe Societies, July 2.

Speech introducing M. Jusserand as British Academy Shakespeare
Lecturer. Public Meeting in Burlington House, July 5.

Speech in Peterhouse Hall. Dinner to Old Members of the College,
July 11.

Short speech in King's College Hall. Luncheon to Association of
Booksellers, July 17.

Withington Girls School. Address on the 25th Anniversary of its
Foundation, July 27.

Ockbrook School Prize Giving. Address, July 31.

Short speech in Peterhouse Hall. Election of Mr Searle as Fellow,
Oct. 30.

Speech in Peterhouse Combination Room. Presentation of Portrait
of A. W. W. to the College, Oct. 30.

Short speech at Annual Dinner of Royal Society, Nov. 30.]

1912

Lord Augustus William Frederick Spencer Loftus.
(*D.N.B.* 2nd Supplement, vol. II.)

William Dalrymple Maclagan, Archbishop of York.
(*D.N.B.* 2nd Supplement, vol. II.)

6-3

Sir Theodore Martin.   (*D.N.B.* 2nd Supplement, vol. II.)

*_The Effects of the Thirty Years' War._ Lecture delivered at the Royal Institution, March 8.

*_Goethe and the French Revolution._ Presidential Address at the Annual Meeting of the English Goethe Society, June 25.
(Goethe Soc. Trans.)

Address at Annual General Meeting of British Academy, July 1.
(Proc. Brit. Acad.)

Presidential Address at British Academy, Oct. 30.
(Proc. Brit. Acad.)

The Gains of Old Age. From the German of W. v. Humboldt.
(The Bazaar, W. A. E. Axon, Manchester, Oct.)

Short notice of 'Metternich,' by G. A. C. Sandeman. 1911.
(E.H.R. Jan.)

Short notice of 'Le Poète Georges Herwegh,' par Victor Fleury. 1911.   (*E.H.R.* Jan.)

Short notice of 'Die Partei Bethmann-Hollweg und die Reaktion in Preussen, 1850–1858,' von Walter Schmidt. 1910.
(E.H.R. Jan.)

Short notice of 'Bericht des Herzogs Ernst II. von Koburg über den Frankfurten Fürstentag, 1863,' von Kurt Dorien. (Historische Bibliothek, XXI.) 1910.   (*E.H.R.* Jan.)

Short notice of 'La Restauration de l'Empire Allemand; le rôle de la Bavière,' par A. von Ruville; traduction par Pierre Albin. 1911.   (*E.H.R.* April.)

Review of 'Histoire de Prusse,' par Albert Waddington. Tome I. 1911.   (*E.H.R.* July.)

Short notice of 'Bismarck und die Hohenzollern Kandidatur,' von Ernst Marx. 1911.   (*E.H.R.* July.)

Short notice of 'Les Origines diplomatiques de la Guerre de 1870–1871,' par Justus Ficker. 1912.   (*E.H.R.* July.)

Short notice of 'Briefwechsel zwischen König Johann von Sachsen und den Königen Friedrich Wilhelm IV. und Wilhelm I. von Preussen.' Ed. by Prince John George of Saxony, with the co-operation of Hubert Ermisch. 1911.   (*E.H.R.* Oct.)

*The Epistolae Obscurorum Virorum. In connexion with 1. 'Epistolae Obscurorum Virorum: the Latin text with an English rendering, notes and an historical introduction,' by Francis Griffin Stokes. 1909.—2. 'Die Verfasser der Epistolae Obscurorum Virorum,' von Walther Brecht. (Quellen und Forschungen zur Sprach- und Kultur-Geschichte der Germanischen Völker, 93.) 1904.—3. 'Ulrichi Hutteni Eq. Operum Supplementum. Epistolae Obscurorum Virorum cum inlustrantibus adversariisque scriptis.' Coll. rec. adnot. Edvardus Böcking. Bde. I–II. 1864–9.   (*Q.R.* Jan.)

The Peterhouse Admissions Book (Dr Walker).
(*Peterhouse Sexcentenary Mag.* Dec.)

Revision of A. W. Holland's "Modern Germany" for Anglo-German Friendship Committee, May.

[Address to Royal Society from British Academy at 250th Anniversary of Foundation of Royal Society. Presented July 16.

Speech at Presentation to Dr and Mrs P. W. Latham in the Hall of Trinity Hall, March 15.

Speech at College Commemoration, May 4.

Speech at dinner of the Fisher Society to Cardinal Bourne, May 6.

Speech in Peterhouse Hall. Count Metternich's Honorary Degree, June 18.]

1913

Presidential Address to British Academy, July 1.

(Proc. Brit. Acad.)

Louise de Prusse, Princesse Antoine Radziwill. Review of 'Quarante-cinq Ans de ma vie (1770 à 1815).' 5me édition. 1912. (Publ. by Princess Castellane-Radziwill.)   (*E.H.R.* Jan.)

Short notice of article on letters of Princess Sophia Dorothea, by R. Geerds in Zeitschrift des historischen Vereins für Niedersachsen, lxxvii, 4.   (*E.H.R.* April.)

Short notice of 'Friedrich Gentz, an opponent of the French Revolution and Napoleon,' by Paul F. Reiff. (University of Illinois Studies in Social Sciences.) 1912.   (*E.H.R.* April.)

Short notice of 'Briefe Heinrichs von Treitschke.' 1912.

(E.H.R. April.)

Short notice of 'Les Origines diplomatiques de la Guerre de 1870–1871,' par Justus Ficker. Tome vi.   (*E.H.R.* April.)

*Review of 'Briefe von und an Friedrich von Gentz'; herausgegeben von Friedrich Carl Wittichen und Ernst Salzer. Bd. iii, Theil i. 1803–1819. 1913.   (*E.H.R.* July.)

*Review of 'Briefe von und an Friedrich von Gentz,' herausgegeben von Friedrich Carl Wittichen und Ernst Salzer. Bd. iii, Theil ii, 1820–1832. 1913.   (*E.H.R.* Oct.)

Short notice of Paper in "Preussische Jahrbücher" (Aug.) on 'Börne and E. T. A. Hoffmann,' by C. Daniels. (*E.H.R.* Oct.)

Short notice of 'Meine Erlebnisse zu hannover'scher Zeit, 1839–1866,' von Julius Hartmann. (Publ. by his son, Hermann Hartmann. 1912.)   (*E.H.R.* Oct.)

The late Lord Gorell of Brampton.

(Peterhouse Sexcentenary Mag. June.)

[Address to the International Historical Congress, Lincoln's Inn Hall, prefatory and supplementary to Lord Bryce's Presidential Address, read by A. W. W. as Acting President, April 3.

International Historical Congress. Speech at Government Banquet, April 4.

International Historical Congress. Speech at Lyceum Club Dinner, April 7.

International Historical Congress. Speech at Final Meeting of Congress, April 9.

International Historical Congress. Speech in Peterhouse Hall, April 10, to Visitors from Congress.

Substance of final Report of the Library Syndicate on the Acton Library, June.

Introductory remarks to Shakespeare Oration by Prof. A. Brandl at British Academy Soirée, July 1.]

1914

A Page in "King Albert's Book," ed. by Hall Caine for the *Daily Telegraph*, Dec.

Short notice of article in "Preussische Jahrbücher," Sept. 18, 1913, on Tortensson, by M. Hobohm.   (*E.H.R.* Jan.)

Short notice of P. Albin's 'La Paix Armée; l'Allemagne et la France en Europe (1885–1894).' 1913.   (*E.H.R.* Jan.)

Review of 'Eduard von Bomhard, ein Lebens- und Charakterbild, verfasst von Ernst von Bomhard.' 1913.   (*E.H.R.* April.)

Review of 'Heinrich von Treitschke's Briefe'; herausgegeben von Max Cornicelius. Bd. II. 1913.   (*E.H.R.* July.)

Short notice of 'Die Flucht des Prinzen von Preussen,' von "Major O."   (*E.H.R.* July.)

Short notice of 'Aus den Tagen Bismarcks,' von Otto Gildemeister. 1913.   (*E.H.R.* July.)

Review of 'Les Origines Diplomatiques de la Guerre de 1870–1871. Recueil de documents publié par la Ministère des Affaires étrangères, tomes VII–IX.' 1913–1914. (*E.H.R.* Oct.)

John Wesley Hales, 1836–1914.   (*Christ's College Mag.* June.)

*James Shirley. Critical Essay and edition of "The Royall Master." (Gayley's Representative English Comedies, vol. III.) New York.

[A few words at Peterhouse Commemoration Dinner, May 16.

A few words at English Goethe Society Dinner, Trocadero Restaurant, May 20.

A few words: College Choristers Sunday School Prize Giving, Alexandra Hall, June 7.

Charles Kingsley. Lecture to Peterhouse Theological and Historical Societies, Dec. 8.

Reception of Belgian Professors and Students at Peterhouse, Dec. 19.

Reports for University Press Syndicate on six works.]

1915

Short notice of H. Welschinger's 'La Protestation de l'Alsace-Lorraine.' 1914.   (*E.H.R.* Jan.)

Review of 'The Legislative Union of England and Scotland,' by P. Hume Brown. (Ford Lectures, 1914.) 1914.
(*E.H.R.* April.)

Review of 'La Guerre de Sept Ans: histoire diplomatique et militaire,' par Richard Waddington. Tome V. 1914. (*E.H.R.* July.)

Short notice of 'Biographical studies in Scottish Church History,' by the Bishop of Aberdeen and Orkney. (*E.H.R.* Oct.)

Sir Henry E. Roscoe. An Appreciation. (*M.G.* Dec. 20.)

[A few words at Presentation of a Bust of Lord Kelvin to Peterhouse, Feb.

A few words at the Presentation of the Librarian's (F. Jenkinson's) Portrait by Sargent to the University Library at Trinity College, Dec. 7.

Reports for the University Press Syndicate on three works.]

1915–24

Annual Peterhouse Record for the years 1914–1923. Issued 1915–1924. Ed. by A. W. W.

1916

1616 *and Earlier Centenaries. (Shakespeare Tercentenary Book of Homage.)*

Review of 'The Silesian Loan and Frederick the Great,' by Sir Ernest Satow. 1915. (*E.H.R.* Jan.)

Short notice of 'Germany since 1740,' by G. M. Priest. 1914–1915. (*E.H.R.* Jan.)

Review of 'The Evolution of Prussia; the making of an empire,' by J. A. R. Marriott and C. Grant Robertson. 1915. (*E.H.R.* April.)

*Review of 'The Second Partition of Poland; a study in diplomatic history,' by Robert Howard Lord. (Harvard Historical Studies, no. XXIII.) 1915. (*E.H.R.* Oct.)

Geoffrey Reynolds Day. (*Cambridge Rev.* Oct. 25.)

In Memoriam. Sidney George Gillum. (*Guardian,* July 13.)

Sir E. Thorpe's "Memoir of Sir H. Roscoe." Review of 'The Rt Hon. Sir Henry Enfield Roscoe: a biographical sketch,' by Sir Edward Thorpe.   (*M.G.* Nov. 15.)

[Report on Essays for Members' Prize (English). Jan. (With G. T. Lapsley.)

Address on Peterhouse to Ely Students (Women), May 6.

Reception of French Professors in Peterhouse Combination Room, June 2.]

1916–18

Germany, 1815–1890. 3 vols. (Cambridge Historical Series.) Vol. III has a contribution by Prof. Spenser Wilkinson. Cambridge.

1917

**Founder's Day in War Time.* (Commemoration Address at Memorial Service for members of the University of Manchester who have fallen in the War, and Commemoration of Founders and Benefactors. Whitworth Hall, March 23.) Manchester.

Review of 'A Guide to Diplomatic Practice,' by the Rt Hon. Sir Ernest Satow. 2 vols. 1917.   (*E.H.R.* July.)

The late Rev. Kenelm H. Smith.   (*The Burian*, Dec.)

James Hoyle. (*The Serpent, Manchester University Mag.* April 21.)

Oswald G. F. J. Breul.
                    (Roll of Honour, *Cambridge Rev.* Oct. 25.)

Lord Acton's Letters. Review of 'Selections from the Correspondence of the first Lord Acton'; ed., with an introduction, by J. N. Figgis and R. V. Laurence. Vol. I.   (*M.G.* Oct. 15.)

[A few words at Presentation of Testimonial to Rev. A. J. C. Allen (St Mary the Less), Dec. 21.]

1918

Review of 'Geschichte Europas von 1848 bis 1871,' von Alfred Stern. Bd. 1. (Geschichte Europas seit den Verträgen von 1815 bis zum Frankfürter Frieden von 1871.) 1916.

(*E.H.R.* Jan.)

Short notice of 'Hugo Grotius; the father of the modern science of international law,' by Hamilton Vrieland. 1917.

(*E.H.R.* July.)

Welcome and Godspeed! (Echoes of 'C' Cadet Battalion, Peterhouse and Downing, June.)

Review of 'The Question of Alsace-Lorraine,' by Jules Dunhem; translated by Mrs R. Stanwell. 1918.

(*Cambridge Rev.* June 6.)

[Recollections of Edward Blount Smith. (For "Family Papers.") Jan.

Report on an application for Degree of D.D., Dec.

Reports for the Syndics of the University Press on six books.]

1919

The Period of Congresses. 3 parts. (Helps for Students of History.)

Securities of Peace. (Helps for Students of History.)

*Shakespeare and the Makers of Virginia. (British Academy Shakespeare Lecture.)

Short notice of 'Armed Neutralities,' ed. by J. Brown Scott, and 'Treaties of 1785, 1799, and 1828 between the United States and Prussia,' ed. by J. Brown Scott.   (*E.H.R.* July.)

The late Sir Chas. Abercrombie Smith.

(*Peterhouse Sexcentenary Mag.* July.)

Professor Dejace. (With his letter from Liége.)

(*Cambridge Rev.* Feb. 14.)

H. G. Aldis.   (*Cambridge Rev.* March 7.)

Obituary. The late Sir Charles Abercrombie Smith.

(*Times Educational Supplement*, May 29.)

[Toast to Sir W. R. Birdwood after dinner in Peterhouse Hall, Feb. 8.

A few words on Dr Barber's Farewell at Leys School, June 27.

Speech in Bury St Edmunds Town Hall on School War Memorial, July 10.

Letter to H. W. V. Temperley on Historical Research, Dec.

Report for the Syndics of the University Press on five books.]

1920

Review of 'Thoughts on the Union of England and Scotland,' by Albert V. Dicey and Robert S. Rait. 1920.   (*E.H.R.* Oct.)

[A few words in Peterhouse Combination Room on Proposed Wellington (N.Z.) War Memorial Chapel, Feb. 16.

Translation of a Report on the Vienna Archives. Read at the Royal Historical Society, Oct.]

1921

Collected Papers: Historical; Literary; Travel and Miscellaneous.
5 vols. Cambridge.   Vol. 1. Historical, i. Contents: 1. The Peace of Europe, 1873. 2. Finlay's History of Greece, 1878. 3. Roman manners under the earlier Emperors, 1864 and 1872. 4. The Hanseatic League, 1864. 5. Elizabeth of Bohemia, 1885. 6. Tilly, 1864. 7. The Empire under Ferdinand III, 1865. 8. Songs of the Thirty Years' War, 1863. 9. The Effects of the Thirty Years' War, 1912. 10. Gardiner's reign of Charles I,

1877 and 1882. 11. Colonel Hutchinson and his wife, 1886. 12. Memoirs of General Ludlow, 1895. 13. Memoirs of Mary II, 1886. 14. Leibniz as a Politician, 1910. 15. Elizabeth, Princess Palatine, 1902.

Vol. II. Historical, ii. Contents: 16. Burton's Reign of Queen Anne, 1880. 17. Godolphin, 1889. 18. Michael's English History in the 18th century, 1897. 19. Köcher's History of Hanover and Brunswick, 1885. 20. The Great Elector, 1898, 1903 and 1905. 21. The Prussian Crown, 1889. 22. Rheinsberg, 1880. 23. Lewis XV and the Reversal of Alliances, 1898. 24. The Outbreak of the Seven Years' War, 1866. 25. The Decline of Prussia under Frederick William II, 1891. 26. Sixtynine years at the Prussian Court (Countess Voss), 1875. 27. The Second Partition of Poland, 1916. 28. The Girlhood of Queen Louisa, 1900. 29. Frederick of Württemberg, 1890. 30. Aims and Aspirations of European Politics in the Nineteenth Century, 1904. 31. Prince Charles Leiningen, 1911. 32. The Letters of Gentz, 1911 and 1913. 33. The Stein Monument, 1875. 34. Hertslet's Map of Europe by Treaty, 1875. 35. Memoirs of Sir Robert Morier, 1911. 36. The Hohenlohe Memoirs, 1906. 37. Lord Bryce on the New German Empire, 1873.

Vol. III. Literary, i. Contents: 1. 'The Ship of Fools,' 1909. 2. The Brethren of Deventer, 1882. 3. Reuchlin, 1871. 4. 'Epistolae Obscurorum Virorum,' 1912. 5. Introduction to the 'Spider and the Flie,' 1894. 6. Some Academical experiences of the German Renascence, 1878. 7. Sir Philip Sidney, 1893. 8. An Elizabethan Traveller (Fynes Moryson), 1903. 9. Part of Introduction to Shakespeare's 'Henry VI,' 1907. 10. Shakespeare and the Makers of Virginia, 1919. 11. Ben Jonson's Prose, 1894. 12. Introduction to 'A Woman killed with kindness,' 1897. 13. James Shirley, 1914. 14. The Parnassus Plays, 1887. 15. The Female Rebellion, 1901. 16. Sir Henry Wotton, 1909.

Vol. iv. Literary, ii. Contents: 17. John Milton Tercentenary Oration, 1908. 18. Benedict Turretini, 1888. 19. Pattison's 'Milton,' 1880. 20. Dryden's Verse, 1880. 21. Evelyn's 'Diary,' 1908. 22. A Study of Good Women, 1892. 23. The Poems of Bishop Ken, 1894. 24. Halifax, 1906. 25. Abraham a Sancta Clara, 1867. 26. The Poems of John Byrom, 1894. 27. Swift's Love Story in German Literature, 1877. 28. Leslie Stephen on Pope, 1880. 29. Lady M. W. Montagu, 1894. 30. Introduction to Lillo's 'London Merchant' and 'Fatal Curiosity,' 1916. 31. Klopstock and his friends, 1868. 32. Creizenach's English Drama (iv. 1), 1909. 33. 'Everyman' at the Charterhouse, 1901. 34. Georg Brandes on Shakespeare, 1898. 35. Goethe and the French Revolution, 1912. 36. Düntzer's 'Life of Goethe,' 1884. 37. Ludwig Börne, 1867. 38. Hillebrand on Modern German Thought, 1880. 39. Dickens as a Social Reformer, 1906. 40. In Memoriam, E. C. Gaskell, 1910.

Vol. v. Travel and Miscellaneous. Contents: 1. Delphi, 1877. 2. Treves, The Belgic Rome, 1863. 3. The Citadel of the German Knights, 1887. 4. The North-Frisian Outlands, 1868. 5. Lübeck, 1865. 6. Cracow and Warsaw, 1868. 7. Saint-Napoléon, 1864. 8. The Intellectual City, 1865. 9. National Self-Knowledge, 1866. 10. The University of Athens, 1876. 11. The Universities and the Counter-Reformation, 1890. 12. Is it expedient to increase the number of Universities in England? 1878. 13. Pi-Pa-Ki, 1879. 14. The Study of History at Cambridge, 1872. 15. The New Tripos, 1883. 16. Jacob Grimm, 1863 and 1864. 17. Karl Ritter, 1886. 18. Ernst Curtius, 1904. †19. The Late Mr E. A. Freeman, 1892 and 1895. 20. The late Lord Acton, 1902. 21. Sir Leslie Stephen, 1904. 22. Alfred Ainger, 1904. 23. The Late Dr Donaldson,

† By inadvertence the obituary notice of E. A. Freeman, written by Prof. T. F. Tout, was reprinted instead of A. W. W.'s leader on E. A. Freeman which appeared in the same issue of the *Manchester Guardian*, March 18, 1892 (see p. 49).

1861. 24. Helen Faucit, 1898. 25. Founders' Day at Manchester in War Time, 1917. 26. The Founder of Peterhouse, 1885. 27. Postscript and Envoi, 1921.

Review of 'Englische Geschichte im achtzehnten Jahrhundert,' von Wolfgang Michael. Bd. II, Theil I. 1920.   (*E.H.R.* April.)

Review of 'Histoire de l'Internationalisme,' par Christian C. Lange. Tome I. (Publications of the Norwegian Nobel Institute, vol. IV.) 1919.   (*E.H.R.* July.)

Germany and her political future. Review of 'Deutsche Briefe und Elsässische Erinnerungen,' von Friedrich Curtius.
(*The Nation and Athenaeum*, Oct. 1.)

The late Bishop W. J. Harrison.   (*The Burian*, March.)

The late Rev. L. D. Agate.   (*The Serpent*, Feb.)

The late Victor Emile Marsden.   (*The Serpent*, March.)

[A few words in Peterhouse Hall after lunch to Members of the Historical Association, Jan. 9.]

1922

Review of 'Wallenstein's Ende.' Ursachen, Verlauf und Folgen der Katastrophe auf Grund neuer Quellen untersucht und dargestellt, von Heinrich, Ritter von Srbik. 1920. (*E.H.R.* July.)

Short notice of Dr Wolfgang Michael's monograph on the Abbé de Saint-Pierre in Meinecke and Oncken's "Klassiker der Politik," 1922.   (*E.H.R.* Oct.)

The late Mr A. R. Waller.   (*Cambridge Rev.* Oct. 13.)

Sir George Prothero.   (*Times*, July 12.)

[The late Lord Bryce. (Sent to Lady Bryce.) June.]

1922–23

The Cambridge History of British Foreign Policy, 1783–1919. Edited by A. W. W. and G. P. Gooch. 3 vols. Cambridge.

The following are by A. W. W.: Vol. I, Introduction (140 pp.). Vol. II, chap. XIII. The Schleswig Holstein Question (1852–1866). Vol. II, chap. XIV. Greece and the Ionian Islands (1832–1864).

1923

Review of 'Geschichte Europas seit den Verträgen von 1815 bis zum Frankfürter Frieden von 1871,' von Alfred Stern. Vol. VIII. (Vol. II of Pt III, 1848–1871.) 1920.   (*E.H.R.* April.)

[A few words in Combination Room to Degree Candidates after breakfast, June 19.

Short speeches at Peterhouse to welcome New Fellows and Scholars, Oct. 29.

Reply to Enquiry from Cambridge University Royal Commission, stating objections to Royal Commission's Report (1922), drafted on behalf of the Master and Fellows of Peterhouse, with suggestions by Fellows, by the Master, assisted by Mr E. C. Francis, and adopted by College Meeting, Dec. 18.]

1924

The Alliance of Hanover. Review of 'The Alliance of Hanover: a study of British Foreign Policy in the last years of George I,' by James Frederick Chance. 1923.   (*Q.R.* Jan.)

Dr William Jack.   (*Peterhouse Sexcentenary Mag.* April.)

A Swiss View of British Foreign Policy. Review of 'England's Europäische Politik im neunzehnten Jahrhundert von den französischen Revolutionskriegen bis zum Tode Palmerstons,' von Heinrich David. 1924.   (*Contemporary Rev.* June.)

From my Confessions (unpublished).

On the desirability of deciding early in life on some particular domain of historical study; and on the changes and chances which prevented the writer from carrying out all that he had planned in this direction.

       Sent to *The Serpent* (Manchester), but never printed.

Review of 'Die Entwicklung der Geschichtswissenschaft in den führenden Werken betrachtet,' von Moriz Ritter. 1919. (With a note by the editor on A. W. W., who died on June 19.)

       (E.H.R. July.)